Margot Cairnes is a highly successful futurist, keynote speaker and the author of five books and hundreds of articles. She is the chairman of Zaffyre, an international leadership consultancy. She is an expert in the development of exceptional organisations and exceptional people in times of rapid change. www.zaffyre.com

STAYING SANE

in a

CHANGING WORLD

A handbook for **work, leadership**
and **life** in the 21st century

MARGOT CAIRNES

BALBOA
PRESS

A DIVISION OF HAY HOUSE

First published in Australasia in 2003 by Simon & Schuster Australia
Design: Graphic Insight Pty Ltd

Balboa Press books may be ordered through booksellers or by contacting:

Balboa Press
A Division of Hay House
1663 Liberty Drive
Bloomington, IN 47403
www.balboapress.com
1-(877) 407-4847

Printed in the United States of America

ISBN: 978-1-4525-3406-0 (sc)
ISBN: 978-1-4525-3407-7 (e)

Balboa Press rev. date: 22 September 2011

I dedicate this book to my daughter, Lija,
whose love, support, faith and goodness
give me so much joy and optimism
for the future of the world.

Acknowledgments

This book has been many years in the making. In 1994 I was asked by Dietrich George, the editor of *Engineers Australia,* to write a column on leadership. The pieces were to be short – around 500 words each. The response to those early articles was strong – both positive and negative. Every month we got letters saying my articles were the best thing in the magazine. We got just as many saying that if 'that woman' was ever published in the magazine again, people would cancel their 30-year membership. Controversy is music to editors' ears. I am still writing my column for *Engineers Australia.* Interestingly, those little articles have gone all around the world, which has led to requests from other editors.

I produced this book in collaboration with my daughter and research assistant, Lija Simpson (a qualified counsellor and life coach); and David Ragg, on whose research several of the articles are based, updated the facts and figures.

In addition, I would like to acknowledge my many guides, teachers and friends, who have given unfailing moral support.

I would also like to acknowledge the following magazines which have published and commissioned the individual articles found in this book: *ACMAD Practice Report*; *BOSS*, the magazine of the *Australian Financial Review*; *CA Charter*, the magazine of the Institute of Chartered Accountants in Australia; *Engineers Australia*, the magazine of the Institute of Engineers Australia; *New Woman; Together;* and *Women and Management*.

Most particularly I would like to thank my readers, many hundreds of whom have sent letters and emails of encouragement, often sharing with me the impact of the articles on them and their lives. The depth of warmth and thought in these messages has certainly helped me to stay sane in a mad world.

Contents

three: CULTURE AND POLITICS

four: PERSONAL DEVELOPMENT

five: LEADERSHIP

six: SPIRITUALITY IN BUSINESS

seven: WOMEN IN BUSINESS

eight: PERSONAL DEVELOPMENT II

nine: SOCIAL ISSUES

Introduction

Everybody knows that the world is changing. We are experiencing change in every part of our lives. Look around and it seems that people everywhere are going slightly mad. Open the newspapers and you'll read things that just a few decades ago were the work of science fiction. We have lost trust in our leaders at work, in politics, and even in our religious life. We worry about our physical safety and that of our children. We see whole economies collapse and worry about our future. We hear endless talk of war and witness heartless acts of terrorism. We are experiencing the large scale devastation of natural disasters. We are constantly stretched by the need to update our skills, or reskill, or just to keep pace with technology as it changes. How, we wonder, are we to stay sane in this mad new world?

Part of the answer to that puzzle is to step back and get our heads around what is happening. To do this we need to review a bit of economic history.

In the 17th century, the world was firmly ensconced in feudalism. People lived in extended family groups in rural communities. Labour was manual. Power rested in the hands of feudal monarchs and lords whose position was supported by the Church. Trades, skills and employment were passed through the family. If your father was a serf, so were you. If your father was the blacksmith, it was because his father was the blacksmith, as was his father before him. Education consisted of on-the-job training. Living and working was close to the land – people were linked to the seasons. Understandably, people thought differently from how we do today. It was a circular, holistic, mystical lifestyle firmly connected to the way of life of their village, their church and their master.

The invention of the machine changed everything. It didn't just change the way people worked the land, it changed the very fundamentals of how people lived, worked and thought. The new industrial technology led to the rise of factories. People flooded into the factories to get work, and whole towns grew around them. Towns became cities. Labour, even rural labour, became automated. With the rise of the towns and cities, extended families were split up, and this, ultimately, led to the rise of the nuclear family. Communities, too, were ruptured as people began to experience urban alienation. Power shifted to the financiers, industrialists, politicians and bureaucrats. The new technology demanded new skills; skills that hadn't previously existed, so they couldn't be passed down through families. This led to the rise of mass education to train people in the new technology. When machines became smarter we saw the rise of mass higher education.

Thinking changed, too. As the machine was the basis of life and work, thinking became mechanical. People started to break everything into bits, study the bits, then recreate the whole, believing they now understood how things worked. The principles underlying Newtonian psychics became a new blueprint for looking at the world. The dominant thinking was that by controlling the environment, outputs could be standardised and productivity increased. This was the science of 'scientific management', which led to the rise of time-and-motion experts. People in the new mechanistic world view were only of use in that they drove the machine. So we became obsessed with observable and measurable human skills, behaviours and competencies, which we then sought to standardise and teach.

Those parts of people that were less visible, less measurable and less controllable, such as emotions and spirit, we sought to ignore, repress and deny. All this worked well for the next several hundred years – until the technology changed again.

**❝ By controlling the environment,
outputs could be standardised
and productivity increased. ❞**

With the rise of information and communication technologies we find ourselves in a new era, an era as different from capitalism as capitalism was from feudalism. Let's call this new era post-capitalism. The new technologies have turned the world into a global village. Markets, corporations and, increasingly, politics now operate as global entities. The inverse of this is cocooning, as people all over the developed world use their wealth and knowledge to create safe cocoons for themselves and their families. House sizes are growing, and within those houses we stock every conceivable comfort and convenience, thus obviating the need to go out. Increasing numbers of people are even working from home.

The nature of work has changed. No longer is the workforce dominated by manual or even automated labour. In the e-world, e-mail and e-business are the norm. The rise of the service sector now accounts for more than half of the GDP in developed countries. With increased mobility, changing values and work patterns, the family too has changed. The nuclear family is breaking down. In some cases it is reforming into blended families, where partners live with assorted children from their current and previous unions. The number of people who live alone is growing, as is the number who will never marry or have children.

In this new e-world, power is shifting away from the nation state to global corporations and rising transglobal political coalitions. The new technology and the speed of change it brings with it demands new ways of learning. So we have now moved into the era of life learning, with people training and retraining constantly. Where in the feudal age a career would pass through six generations, in the post-capitalist world, increasing numbers of individuals are experiencing six careers in one lifetime.

With all this change, our thinking too needs to evolve. What I see all over the world is people living in the e-world and thinking in machine-age ways. This book of articles provides e-world ways of looking at a whole variety of issues – from work to leadership, to spirituality and to family life. It provides not a mechanistic blueprint of the way ahead, but a virtual prompt for those seeking to make sense of post-capitalism as it evolves.

Feudalism	Capitalism	Post-Capitalism
Country	Towns/cities	Global village/cocooning
Manual labour	Automation	E-business, services
Community/extended family	Nuclear family	Singles and blended families
Feudal lords/church	Financiers/industrialists/ MPs, bureaucrats	Corporations
Trades	Mass education	Life learning
Land-based thinking	Linear/machine-age thinking	E-world thinking – holistic, virtual, new science

Staying sane in a mad world involves looking at things differently, asking different questions, allowing our thinking to change with the times. This book of essays is a companion guide to this process.

Living in one era and using thinking patterns and behaviours from a time past creates craziness. When change is extremely rapid, this madness is accentuated, hard to understand and thus difficult to bear. Designed to help you stay sane in a mad world, this book contains articles about various topics. Once you have read the book as a whole you may find yourself going back to the articles that are pertinent to your situation. My aim is to provide you with affirmation (it's the world that is mad, not you), thought provocation (helping you see and think differently) and gentle guidance (through structured questions, advice and skills) to help you survive and thrive in the post-capitalist world.

I have been working for nearly two decades helping business leaders make the transition into the new era. What I have found is that while sanity demands that we shift our thinking, we can't do this without involving both our emotions and our spirit. The questions at the end of each article have been devised with this in mind. While the articles seek to stimulate thought and provide new ways forward, the questions are aimed at helping you make the shift. This will only happen if you take the time to read the articles then answer the questions – taking time to ponder on each one and search your memory and emotions for the answers that make sense to you.

As we begin to adopt e-world thinking, we come to realise that this is an extremely exciting and creative time to be alive. When things change rapidly, both risks and opportunities are created. *Staying Sane in a Changing World* is aimed at supporting you to capture these opportunities by moving sanely into the new era.

one

WORK

Leading the way in the 21st century

Relationship and personal transformation are the keys to strategic success in a rapidly changing world.

On a recent world trip, I visited colleagues working in the field of business and social research to discuss how business can lead the way in the 21st century. The message was strong and consistent, and best summed up by John Naisbitt (author of the *Megatrends* series of books) with the popular phrase, 'Think globally, act locally'. The experts agreed. As the world is becoming smaller, and innovation and information ever more accessible, the places to achieve radical competitive advantage are close to home. Competitive advantage comes through each of us developing our own potential and our strategic and personal relationships.

It is the very rapidity of change that will make relationship and personal transformation the keys to strategic success. Information technology makes data instantaneously available to anyone who wants it. The pace of step–gain is determined by how quickly and effectively organisations make use of that data and incorporate it into their ways of thinking and operating. At the same time as we scan the world for information, we need to be adapting our own ways of thinking, operating and relating so we can make speedy and optimum use of what we find.

The trick here is that we are much better at scanning the environment than we are at changing our thinking, learning new ways of behaving and making our relationships work. Furthermore, while gaining information operates from the outside in, changing ourselves works the other way.

We are conscious of less than 10 per cent of our own thoughts, feelings, psychological responses and body memories. It is almost as if we are running our lives on remote control, which is fine when we can programme the course ahead and the destination. But in changing times this is obviously impossible. What will the banking industry look like in ten years? – the experts say it's beyond current imagination. What about telecommunications or manufacturing? Less than half the workforce in the industrialised world is working in what used to be considered a 'proper' fulltime job. People are expected to operate at a level of performance that is daunting. Many people deny change, others get angry, and others depressed. I find it all very exciting.

> **Personal growth requires time for reflection, courage to face what we discover and ongoing personal support.**

If we need a step-change in our performance, and if relationship and personal growth are the key to ongoing success, then the fact that we are using less than 10 per cent of our potential presents us with a wonderful opportunity. While organisations around the world are tinkering with incremental changes, we possess an untapped treasure-trove of possibility which is almost limitless. There are, however, a few catches.

Tapping our inner resources requires different skills and ways of looking at things other than scanning the world for emerging trends and data. Personal growth requires time for reflection, courage to face what we discover, and ongoing personal support, preferably from a trained professional. Moreover, there is no real personal change without emotional involvement. The uncharted waters of our mind, body and spirit are found through a journey both cognitive and emotional.

Questions to ask yourself

1. The global business community is presently undergoing rapid change in every area. What changes are currently taking place in your organisation/industry?
2. How do you feel about these changes?
3. Great change brings great opportunities. How are you going to use these changes to get more of what you want in life?
4. What support measures are you putting in place to help you capitalise on change? (Examples include a mentor, life coach or professional support group, upgrading your skills, looking after your own personal health, keeping a journal and meditating.)

Changes in the way we work

*Lifelong employment is out – we must now
manage our own careers.*

Charles Handy in *Hungry Spirit* made the observation that around
half (51 per cent) of the UK workforce and around 37 per cent of
the US workforce are now considered temporarily employed –
permanent jobs for them can be simply a string of six-year positions
within corporations. In an interview in *Inc Magazine* (Hopkins et
al.), the two co-authors of *Corporate Cultures: The Rites and Rituals
of Corporate Life*, Terrence Deal and Allan Kennedy, said:

*The traditional corporate culture consisted of an implicit deal
between the company and its employees. You joined the company
and accepted its ethic and standards – its way of life. Then, if you
kept your nose clean and performed reasonably well – according
to how good performance was defined in that organisation – the
company provided you with a nice, comfortable middle-class life.
That was the deal. You committed to the company, the company
committed to you.*

Then came the 1980s and 90s. Shareholders emerged as a company's
chief constituency, and the stock price became king. This led to
downsizing, outsourcing, and the rapid increase in short-term
management thinking. More recently this has been reflected in
the merger boom. As stock-option plans became the primary
mode of paying senior executives, and as stock prices began their

climb, perfectly competent managers quickly realised that they could earn extraordinary sums of money, not by making decisions that were necessarily good for the company, its employees or its customers in the long term, but by doing whatever would make the stock price jump the most.

A major consequence of all those developments is that the old patriarchal deal between the company and its employees is off. Now there's no deal. Top management looks after itself and employees have to do the same.

Dr Peter Brain from the National Institute of Economic and Industry Research in Australia predicts that we are headed for a 30-40-30 society over the next two decades – 30 per cent will be high-income or two-income households in highly skilled full-time employment; 40 per cent will be characterised by spasmodic episodes of full-time employment, long periods of unemployment and episodes of part-time and casual work; the remaining 30 per cent will have little involvement in the labour market with their income dependent upon a combination of social security and limited-duration part-time or casual work.

> **The old patriarchal deal between the company and its employees is off. Now there's no deal.**

Handy echoes Brain's three-tier workforce. He posits, however, that many in tier one – the highly paid executives and professionals – will want to play that game only for a short time. While a jetsetting international life sounds glamorous, the demands of global competition and short-term management thinking quickly lead to burnout, and the cost to health, family and social life can quickly become intolerable. However, after a stint in tier one, many people move voluntarily into tier two. Winners in this tier, while not necessarily as rich as those in tier one, at least have a life with the time to enjoy the benefits of their successes.

Questions to ask yourself

1. What significant changes have you experienced in your work life over the course of your career?
2. How have you dealt with these changes?
3. Do you think that the approach you have taken to dealing with these changes has served you well, or is there a more effective approach you could adopt in the future?

Rediscovering trust and loyalty

*Corporations must reinvent themselves to lift
their poor image and regain our trust.*

A *Business Week* survey (Bernstein) reveals that 72 per cent of those questioned believed corporations have too much power, while 66 per cent think large profits are more important to big companies than developing safe, reliable, quality products for consumers. Alan Greenspan, chairman of the US Federal Reserve Bank, backed up these findings by saying: "At home and abroad, citizens facing globalisation worry that powerful corporations override national sovereignty and can undermine political and monetary systems" (Bernstein).

A Grey Advertising and Sweeney Research survey (quoted by J. Menadue in the *Australian Financial Review*) conducted in February 2000 shows that only 20 per cent of Australians trust big companies. The least trusted are banks, advertising agencies, and petrol, insurance and medical companies. The extent of this disenchantment with big business is clearly reflected in the popular media. American movies, such as *Antitrust, Vertical Limit, Erin Brockovich* and *The Insider,* portray business leaders as greedy, egotistical villains who are prepared to do whatever it takes to gain more personal power and wealth. In Australia, movies such as *The Man Who Sued God* and *The Bank* were also warmly received by the public. In some cinemas, a line in *The*

Bank, "I guess I just hate banks", received shouts of approval and applause from the audience.

> ❝ **The overwhelming response by people to this growing distrust of their leaders is a deep sense of powerlessness.** ❞

It seems that distrust of business is not limited to outsiders – insiders, those who work within the company, don't fare very well either. A 2001 joint Australian Institute of Management and Monash University study of more than 2000 managers showed that they felt their staff simply didn't trust them. They felt they scored badly in terms of loyalty as well.

The overwhelming response by people to this growing distrust of their leaders is a deep sense of powerlessness. When you can't trust the people who are supposed to lead and protect you, who can you trust? If the leaders are unreliable, where do you turn for direction?

Prior to September 11 2001, there was a growing world movement of protest against big business and big government. Since then this voice has been largely silenced. The fear of terrorism has made our current leaders look better than the external enemy. There is nothing like an external threat to silence internal dissent. If you can label demonstrators as terrorists, then you can also create the implication that dissent brings about the same fate suffered by al-Qaeda fighters.

When you silence dissent, though, it doesn't go away; it goes underground, only to reappear in more hostile, less manageable forms. Open systems – those that survive over time – are constantly embracing new information, are self-organising and, thus, are regenerating. Closed systems (such as Communism) shut down and die.

In order to be sustainable, organisations will need to regain the trust of the public; they will need to listen to the dissenting voices of the public and restructure the way they do business.

Questions to ask yourself

1. What do you see is the value of trust and loyalty in the workplace in a time when rapid changes are taking place in the business community?
2. Think of times you have been in trust-filled relationships. What helped to build and maintain this trust?
3. What can you learn from those trust-filled relationships and how can you use what you learnt to build and maintain trust in your relationships at work and at home?

The non-profit drivers

Sometimes the best things in life are free.
Just ask any non-government organisation.

The not-for-profit sector is on the rise and accounts for 29 million full-time (equivalent) jobs, or about one job in every twenty, and contributes an estimated global value of US$1.1 trillion. In 1999, the number of non-government organisations (NGOs) with operations in more than one country was 26,000 - up from 6,000 in 1990. At a time when business, government and media are losing people's trust, the NGO sector is growing at about four times the rate of other sectors.

An Edelman Public Relations worldwide survey in 2000 of opinion leaders in Australia, France, Germany, the UK and the US found that NGOs were trusted nearly twice as much to 'do what is right' than government, media or corporations. More than half the respondents claimed that NGOs 'represent values I believe in'. NGOs ranked much higher as a source of credible information than media outlets or companies on issues including labour and human rights, genetically modified food, the environment and health.

> **❛NGOs attract goodwill, time and energy for free.❜**

My first job out of university was managing an NGO with about 60 paid staff and several hundred volunteers. I answered to eleven community-based committees and three levels of government.

The politics involved were challenging, yet we managed to achieve so much with few financial resources. My next job was lecturing at a university where, again, so much was achieved with so little. When I later moved out into the business world, I never forgot the capacity of NGOs to attract goodwill, time and energy for free. I also never forgot the exhaustion, the politics and the great feeling of satisfaction.

How do NGOs throughout the world get people to work for free or very little, under conditions that are less than fantastic? Here's how:

- NGOs fully realise they are working with volunteers. You can't buy commitment, energy and motivation.
- The push in business to get the employees to own the business is a mainstay principle of NGOs. As the managing director of an NGO, I was accountable to my public. People had no difficulty in letting me know, at any hour of the day or night, what they wanted, and my job was to respond, ensuring that I stayed on my toes, kept close to my public and realised that my place was to serve my stakeholders and their interests – no distant shareholder annual general meetings for me. I was accountable to the board members – they were accountable to the people who elected them.
- NGOs work for the common good, so people willingly go the extra mile. This breeds a palpable spirit of belonging.
- NGOs promote servant leadership. As managing director I had very little direct power, but a huge amount of influence. My influence came through supporting my staff and committees to learn and grow so that they could all do their jobs better. Another huge source of influence came via working with the volunteers, training them and ensuring that they felt appreciated and rewarded for their efforts.
- Everyone is doing the impossible with the invisible; mutual support and encouragement is widespread.

- There is huge satisfaction in providing the community with a greatly needed service.

In summary, the success of NGOs, something that business and government could do well to emulate, lies in their capacity to recognise that their business is people – people in the organisation and people in the community. Plant equipment and financial resources are there to serve people. Operating from this stance, it is amazing how much can be achieved inexpensively, ensuring there are a lot more resources to spread around at the end of the day. Is there any business that couldn't learn from this model?

Questions to ask yourself
1. What do you think you can learn from the principles that make NGOs successful?
2. Why do you think it is so important for organisations to value their staff?
3. What helps you to feel valued for the work you do?
4. What can you do to help others feel valued for their work?

Surviving super mergers

*Mergers pose the challenge of acclimatising to a new culture,
new workmates, new systems and new procedures.*

We are in the era of the super merger: BP/Amoco, Citibank/
Travellers, BT/Deutsche Bank, etc. Lumbering giants across the
globe are getting even bigger. For those employed by companies
rushing headlong into corporate marriages, these mergers are
revolutionising their lives.

Some people find they no longer have a job. Others are being
relocated. When BP Oil Europe merged with Mobil Oil Europe,
many executives transferred from one company to the other.
This meant leaving a company they had been with since school
– that is, for periods of twenty, 30 or even more years. One Mobil
executive seconded to BP Oil Europe told me: 'I have been so much
a company man. Mobil corporate colours were red and blue. These
were the colours that ran through my veins. Now, after 30 years'
service, you cut me and I have to bleed green and gold.'

For those who retain their jobs there is the challenge of
acclimatising to a new culture, new workmates, new systems and
new procedures. For many executives this may well mean having
to forge relationships with people thousands of kilometres away.
Lobbying to have your part of the organisation retained, looked
after or sold with dignity can call for hundreds of hours flying
around the globe to meet new owners. For executives in outposts,
merging often means negotiating new terms of employment
with strangers. This means that on top of grieving for their lost
colleagues, fretting over their job security, having to learn a whole

new way of operating and fighting to retain their right to do business, executives from merging companies are also highly likely to be suffering from jetlag.

Spending time talking with such executives, I am constantly struck by the impact these changes have on people's thinking. Tired, grieving executives, who are fighting for their jobs and the existence of companies they have built, rarely think or act at their best. The temptation to revert to reactionary, knee-jerk behaviour is huge. The strategic skills that led to prior success seem to fade as they fight exhaustion, chaos and fear.

In this environment, how can profits be greatly increased, strategic improvements be made and enduring relationships be forged? How does the business continue to function at all? When I have asked executives from merged companies these questions, they admit they are stressed to superhuman limits. They then start babbling out a rationale in some strange economic jargon that obviously helps them to make sense of the insanity of their situation. Finally, they note that everybody else is in the same boat. A picture comes to mind of lemmings following each other over a cliff. Don't think, don't question and don't ask why. Just follow the leader. That seems to be the way to survive.

> **❝ Tired, grieving executives, who are fighting for their jobs and the existence of companies they have built, rarely think or act at their best. ❞**

If survival means keeping a highly paid corporate job in the short term, they are probably right. If survival means staying healthy, staying married, staying sane and doing good business, then one has to question the sanity behind merger mania. We can no longer expect to work in the same organisation for our whole lives. This means that we need to be able to adjust to new cultures, new workmates, new systems and new procedures.

Questions to ask yourself

Think of a time when you were first introduced to a new work environment with new rules and new relationship dynamics.

1. How did you feel about this new experience?
2. What support structures did you put in place for yourself, such as regular massages, going to the gym, finding a mentor, coach, counsellor, supportive friends/family?
3. What would you like to do differently next time you are in this situation to make your transition easier?

Don't do anything – you might make a mistake

In bureaucracies, action can bear the risk of making a mistake and embarrassing political masters.

It is a truism in any large bureaucracy that it is better to do nothing than to take the risk of action, since when you act you might make a mistake. While you remain idle you can't possibly do anything wrong, therefore you won't get a black mark against your name. All this rests on the belief that those who get ahead are not the most competent, effective and best leaders, but rather those with the fewest black marks.

Now this line of reasoning has much to commend it. Modern leadership theory expounds the value of honesty, integrity and relationship. Leaders are encouraged to listen, and to create safe environments in which issues can be raised and openly discussed, problems solved, and goals set and monitored. All this is premised on the idea that organisations operate to create social or economic wealth, to perform necessary functions and to meet socially and economically beneficial objectives.

It has been my experience over the years that all this has very little to do with government bureaucracy, for reasons that have practically nothing to do with bureaucrats and everything to do with the dynamics of the political systems. Moreover, the gatekeepers of ineffective government are those watchdogs of public opinion, the media.

Let's have a look at the way the system works. Politicians, in order to maintain power, need to make the decisions they believe to be important to ensure re-election. They need the public to believe they are good, honest representatives who care about their constituents and are competent to handle the issues of government. To maintain their public standing, MPs need to project a public-relations image that is likely to win and maintain voters' support.

> **The role of bureaucracy, therefore, is to save face for the current set of political masters.**

The media's role in all this is that they can make or break the public image of anyone in public office. Moreover, as the media prefers to give coverage to controversial issues, journalists are constantly looking for stories about failures, misjudgments and mistakes. The opposition parties are only too keen to be obliging in providing the media with any evidence they need of blundering on the part of a political rival. This sets up a dynamic where politicians (and especially those in power) do everything not to rock the boat, not to make mistakes and not to be seen in anything but the best public light.

As those in government are in effect the key figures of governance in the public sector, they are the transmitters of the strongest cultural messages. They, through their actions and demeanour, set the social and emotional atmosphere in the realms over which they rule. The message they send is loud and clear: 'Don't make any embarrassing mistakes. Remember, appearances are everything.'

The role of bureaucracy, therefore – despite all the propaganda, all the dedication of public servants and all the hard work of lobby groups – is to save face for the current set of political masters. I can't tell you how many department heads have told me the anguish of not doing what made social and business sense because what worked for the common good might upset some key constituents of a powerful minister. Working in the top reaches of government bureaucracy is like working in a goldfish bowl. Everything you do is on show; looking good matters more than getting on with something of value.

This can only be highly demoralising, not to mention horrifically wasteful of public monies, and hopelessly ineffective for the social and economic good of the nation. In such an environment the stereotype of the faceless public servant makes incredibly good sense. He is just following the minister's example and doing what he is paid to do: working to preserve the minister's public image.

Questions to ask yourself

1. It is only by taking risks that we are able to reach our goals. In your own life, do you take the risk of acting upon your dreams? If not, what do you think it is that stops you from taking risks?
2. What one goal or dream do you have that would improve your personal or work life? What are you doing to achieve this goal?

Busy isn't necessarily productive

Psychological, physical and spiritual health is good for strategic thinking, action and relationships.

At an international banking conference I addressed recently, the delegates were discussing the impossibility of doing their jobs without working twelve- to fourteen-hour days. They were expected to be seen to be busy and, in spite of all the forms, procedures, plans and budgets, they usually had to process added hours onto their 'real jobs' to indicate 'busyness'. My suggestions that they spend more time looking after their psychological, physical and spiritual health were met with a chorus of, "It's all right for you, you're self-employed." No amount of argument would have them believe that by being happy, healthy and relaxed they would be in a better place to conduct their relationships and have sufficient perspective to think strategically.

Then one of the delegates told us that he had needed to visit a variety of areas of his bank to oversee the implementation of some new procedures. To do this he had had to spend a considerable amount of time with various section leaders, all but one of whom held the belief that they had to work long days filled with constant visible activity. The dissenting leader believed that what mattered was what he and his people achieved, not how busy they were. This guy's usual pattern was to come to work at 9am and leave at 5pm. It turned out that he had the most successful section in the bank.

He continually surpassed his objectives, was adored by his people and was definitely on the bank's high-flyers fast-track.

Apparently this leader knew very clearly what he wanted. He explicitly prioritised his objectives and focused on two or three key issues at a time. He always worked to achieve precisely defined and widely communicated outcomes, and concentrated strongly on developing relationships with the people who could help him achieve these outcomes. In other words, he knew what he wanted and he concentrated his efforts on getting it, rather than doing what other people might think he should be doing. My guess is this also allowed him to be his own man, and it obviously allowed him to have a life outside of work, something denied to those working 70- to 80-hour weeks and who openly admitted they were just too tired to do or even think about anything but work.

Of course, setting your objectives and focusing your energy on achieving them takes a lot of courage. We all have a tendency to operate like sheep, blindly adhering to the cultural norms of our organisations, even when these shared habits are patently silly and dysfunctional. I remember working with a network of people in an organisation when the collective response to downsizing was for everybody to work longer and longer hours, while apparently achieving less and less. Someone described it as musical chairs. If you weren't there looking busy when the music stopped, you mightn't get a seat. So everybody just hung around looking busy, guarding their rear.

The network members agreed they were probably less than 20 per cent productive, so they collectively decided to work fewer and more productive hours, keeping each other informed of relevant data and providing each other with emotional and political support. It is not surprising that their health, marriages and personal happiness improved, as did their individual effectiveness. When disaster struck – the organisation underwent a major political upheaval accompanied by massive retrenchments – some of these people decided to leave and went on to better jobs elsewhere. The majority of them were promoted. Balance, clearly focused energy and supportive relationships enabled them to survive and thrive where many of their 'busy'-looking colleagues floundered.

❝ **Setting your objectives and focusing your energy on achieving them takes a lot of courage.** ❞

Questions to ask yourself

1. Do you maintain a good balance between your personal and work life?
2. How do you help yourself to work smarter, not longer, hours? What else could you do?
3. What steps do you take to ensure you look after your personal relationships and physical, emotional and spiritual health, such as putting dates in your diary to go the gym or to go for walks, making regular dates with family and friends, signing up for a regular health class?

Work can be fun and a place of growth

Heroic workplaces allow people to be true to themselves, to their own talent and to their own values.

Leading playwright David Williamson sent me tickets to his play *Corporate Vibes*, which was an hilarious account of workplace relationships gone mad. Williamson had modelled the key characters in his play on stereotypes that I had developed in my book *Approaching the Corporate Heart*, in which I talk about warriors (old-style leaders) and heroes (a modern alternative). Warriors are machine-age thinkers who try to control everyone and everything, deny change and concentrate on making money regardless of the human, ethical or environmental costs. Heroes have made the shift to e-world thinking; they are masters at understanding and working with paradox, change and the reality of human emotion and spirit, not at the expense of profits but so they can enrich everybody – including themselves – while taking into account their responsibility for the social and physical environment. Williamson had been fascinated by bizarre behaviour he had seen in the corporate world and was looking for a way of dramatising it. He had wandered into a bookshop and seen my then newly released book. He took it home, loved it, and used its concepts as an impetus to create fictional characters and circumstances that brought the concepts to life.

Corporate Vibes depicts a typical second-wave warrior (property developer Sam Siddons), whose company is on the verge of bankruptcy mostly because of Sam's egotistical refusal to listen to the advice of the people he employs. Sam's response to this situation is to demand that his top staff members be sacked and replaced with people who can give him the advice he wants to hear. 'I want,' declares Sam, 'staff who are willing to bleed for me.'

Sam's main problem in sacking his top personnel is his new human resource director, Deborah, an Aboriginal woman hired to make the equal-opportunity audit figures look better.

To Sam's great dismay, Deborah has managed to negotiate a contract that gives her final say over hire and fire. She flatly refuses to sack anyone without good reason – something she thinks Sam lacks. Instead of doing Sam's bidding she sets about freeing up the creative energy and performance potential of the people around her. For Deborah, "work should be creative and fulfilling, not a prison sentence". A true hero, she gets the staff to contact their own sense of purpose, unleash their personal power and bring all this into relationship with their work. That means into relationship with Sam.

There is another way to do business – an heroic way.

The ensuing debacle has the audience rolling in the aisles. We have all been there before. We have all had a boss like Sam. We have all secretly desired to stand up to him the way that Deborah does. Williamson shows us that there is another way to do business – an heroic way. A way that allows people to be true to themselves, to their own talent and to their own values. A way that works. A way that most warriors fight.

"Business," spits out Sam, "is war. There are no holds barred and no prisoners taken and if you're beaten no one gives a damn. Love? The last person who was stupid enough to say "Love thine enemies" got nailed up."

But even warriors can change once they experience the benefits of working with alive, empowered people striving to meet a common aim. As Sam admits in the final scene of the play, life has been much more fun since his new human resource director was hired. Instead of being surrounded with submissive sycophants he has staff members who are real, alive, creative and fun. The changes in the people around him lead Sam to experience a different dimension of his own personality. Even the fiercest warrior, deep inside, has a human face.

For me, watching *Corporate Vibes* was an eerie experience. Williamson kindly acknowledged the impact *Approaching the Corporate Heart* had upon *Corporate Vibes*. The human resources director often spoke my words. One of my friends commented that Deborah even wore similar clothes to me. She had a similar body language. We learn early on that this is Deborah's first job. As a professional I was very aware of her naivety and lack of skill. I was also confronted with seeing an image of myself as a professional novice. What was really exciting was seeing an audience of 800 people being introduced to concepts that hold so much potential for liberating people's energy and personal wellbeing.

What *Corporate Vibes* teaches, with humour, is that work can be fun, enlivening and a place of growth. Williamson shows us that when we embark on the hero's quest in the workplace we can be more successful, and even the oldest, most warlike dog can learn new tricks and enjoy doing so.

Questions to ask yourself

1. Do you find you are able to be true to yourself, to your talent and to your own values at work?
2. How would you be different at work if you felt more supported to be yourself?
3. Name one change you could make to the way you are at work so you can be truer to yourself and to your talent?

two
WORK
RELATIONSHIPS

Relationships – what are they?

Get more from relationships by looking at them differently.

For years I have urged people to build their relationships. For years they have told me that they already do that – or have looked at me as if I just fell out of a tree. When I looked at their companies and their relationships with their staff, their shareholders and their clients, I saw relationships that were extremely poor. However, when I mentioned this I was generally dismissed.

I found this whole situation so puzzling I have gone on a search to find out why people respond in this way.

First, I discovered that people have very low expectations when it comes to relationships. Most people have had bad relationships with most people most of their lives. Now, before you get cranky with me, just think about it. Our divorce statistics are around one in two. Figures on family violence, alcoholism and other addictions such as gambling and eating disorders make your 'normal' family of mum, dad and a couple of kids living together happily very much an endangered species. According to family therapist Virginia Satir, only about four per cent of the population grow up in families that are 'functional' – appropriate for the emotional, psychological, physical wellbeing and growth of their members. If you have experienced really good relationships you are, statistically, a freak.

Secondly, I worked out that when I suggested people work on their relationships, they heard a whole lot of things that had very little to do with what I was suggesting. Many people think working on your relationships – especially in business – means giving the other person what they want. I enjoyed a very inspirational speech at a conference a few years ago about how Sydney won the 2000 Olympic bid through 'relationship marketing'–which translated to finding out the likes, peccadillos and weaknesses of the IOC members and then pandering to them. More recently, similar behaviour has been represented to us less glamorously as corruption. For me, working on relationships means creating a climate where people can grow on every level, while working together in a collegiate environment, where people grow to respect and care for each other while cooperating to ensure top performance and financial return. This is hard work; hard rewarding work. It isn't about being a sycophant, a yes-man or a con. Quite the contrary. It's about being true to yourself – being courageous enough to deal honestly with the good and bad in each issue and emotionally mature enough to be honest with yourself and others about your agenda, your strengths and your weaknesses. In an environment like that, corruption just isn't possible.

Finally, I found that people couldn't hear me because they didn't want to. It's not that people don't like the dream of having a healthy, growth-inducing, productive work environment – we all like the platitudes – it was that the personal risk involved in making the changes seemed to be too great. The truth is, most people would rather stay somewhere uncomfortable, unproductive and known than move towards something better and unknown.

> ❝ **If you have experienced really good relationships you are, statistically, a freak.** ❞

Joel Barker, in his videotape *The Business of Paradigms*, tells us that when the paradigm changes everybody goes back to zero. The people living in the old system can't even see the new. That is, they are so unskilled in the new model they don't even know what they don't know. For most people this level of ignorance is so terrifying they flip into denial. They don't even try and see the new. Which is why so many great inventors have been tortured, gaoled and cast out. Better to shoot the messenger than admit you have something – even something extremely valuable – to learn.

Questions to ask yourself

Healthy relationships are made possible when all parties involved work at making them successful. Think about a healthy relationship you have been part of or you have witnessed.

1. What qualities did this relationship have?
2. How did you/the people involved in that relationship work at building and maintaining the relationship?
3. Is there anything you could learn from this relationship which would help to improve your current relationships?

Relationships are everything

Interaction is the key to successful leadership.
There's just one catch – you have to use your emotions.

An article titled 'Who Leaders Are', published in the June 1999 issue of *Fast Company* - one of the most successful magazines in the world - listed twelve descriptors of outstanding leaders, including: leaders are authentic, leaders are listeners, and leaders make change happen and stand for values that don't change. Descriptor number five read: 'Leaders make unexpected connections. They organise and lead conversations among people who don't normally interact with each other, and they see the kinds of patterns that allow for small innovation and breakthrough ideas.'

Many people are frightened of their emotions and have shut them down. Yet unless we come to terms with our emotions, we simply do not think straight, let alone strategically.

Outstanding leaders know how to work relationships of thought, personal interaction and organisation to create new ways forward, new answers, new opportunities, new perspectives. Leading people into an unknown future is a frightening responsibility when, by definition, discontinuous change means that we cannot rely on trends from the past to guide the way forward. We can no longer rely on the principles of scientific management which preached cause-and-effect linkages. Now we have to rearrange paradoxes using our intuition and radically honed perception.

Many strategy experts tell us that when strategy is a *static* form of analysis, resulting in a blueprint for action, it is just too slow and out of date for today's world. Leaders need to be constantly expanding their thinking, translating their new world view into action and relating strategically.

Outstanding leaders in times of rapid change build strong, robust relationships, raise their awareness of themselves, of others and of their environment and grow personally in terms of self-confidence, emotional maturity and the ability to relate on a dynamic and meaningful level. They create meaning from paradox and from rapidly changing patterns.

To be outstanding in the future, leaders must adopt leader-ship philosophies based on leading-edge scientific knowledge. Margaret Wheatley, in her groundbreaking book *Leadership and the New Science,* informs us that in the quantum physics world, relationship is everything. The lesson here for leaders is that it is in how ideas, people, energies and events interact that tomorrow's possibilities for quantum improvement lie.

Chaos theory tells us that little changes lead to gigantic shifts – a butterfly flapping its wings on one side of the world can lead to a tornado on the other side of the globe. When translated, this means that as leaders we need to be attuned to subtleties – subtleties of human behaviour, personality, spirit and belief, subtleties of energy shifts and subtleties of events and how they interact.

Systems theory tells us that if you change one part of any system, the whole system changes, as does every system to which that system is connected. For leaders, this means we need to be highly attuned to the dynamics of relationship.

To operate on this level of dynamics, relationships and subtlety, leaders have to radically upgrade their skills of thinking and perception. But herein lies the rub. Our machine- age training has taught us that everything is a skill. Every skill can be broken down into its bits, learnt, understood rationally and put back together to make a totally comprehensible whole. Not so in our e-world.

In *Teaching Thinking,* lateral thinker Edward de Bono tells us that good thinking involves using our emotions and feelings as well as our minds. This expands both the depth and breadth of our thinking, allowing us to be more adept at processing information quickly, practically and laterally. Another expert, Daniel Goleman, tells us in *Emotional Intelligence* that our emotions not only affect our thinking capacity and strength, but they also help us to manage our relationships and keep us up-to-date with rapid change and information explosion.

Now emotions are tricky things. We rarely associate them with good thinking. Many people are frightened of their emotions and have shut them down. Yet unless we come to terms with our emotions, we simply do not think straight, let alone strategically. Emotions are messy, uncontrollable and highly personal. Our emotions are greatly influenced by our unconscious beliefs. The rule of thumb is: that which is unconscious rules us, while we have some choice over that which is conscious.

So learning to be an outstanding leader in times of discontinuous change means learning to bring more emotion into our thinking. This is a challenge for those of us raised and trained in the machine era. Where we were taught to lock away the very parts of our being (our emotions), these now become essential parts of our leadership repertoire. To become outstanding leaders, we need to be emotionally, spiritually and intellectually switched on, which means we need to unlearn years of early socialisation, much of which is unconscious.

Questions to ask yourself

Chaos theory tells us that little changes lead to gigantic shifts – a butterfly flapping its wings on one side of the world can lead to a tornado on the other side of the globe.

1. Have you ever experienced one small change in your life which has then resulted in major changes in other parts of your life?
2. Are there any small changes you could make that would improve your life in a big way?

Two to tango

*Why demanding change from others may not be the
most productive path to corporate bliss.*

I was recently asked, 'How can middle managers like us make
a difference? We are wedged in the middle of the hierarchy. We
don't have any power.' This reminded me of a chief executive
officer who claimed that if he could only find and kill the bloke
called 'senior management', everything in the company would be
fine. Whenever anything went wrong or people felt powerless it
was blamed on the mythical being known as 'senior management'.
But senior managers will tell you that they are powerless because
of the board, the unions and the markets.

Our machine-age training has taught us that answers
are outside of ourselves – visible and measurable. When our
relationships aren't working – when we feel blocked by others
in achieving our aims – we think that the problem is the other
person, therefore the way to amend the situation is to get the other
person to change. We do this by focusing on what we can see
and measure – that is, overt behaviour and response. Our failed
attempts to 'influence others' leave us feeling powerless.

Why do we think that getting others to change behaviour
that annoys us (not them) has even a slight chance of success?
Think about your own attempts to voluntarily change your own
behaviour – for example, to give up smoking, go on a diet, go off
the grog.

❝ **We think that the problem is the other person, therefore the way to amend the situation is to get the other person to change.** ❞

The new sciences as seen in the previous discussions tell us that what matters isn't the things we can see but the relationships between things and people. And this means a sure-fire way to empower ourselves is by having our relationships work in a way that meets our needs. The heroic rule of relationship in my book *Approaching the Corporate Heart* states:

We are all responsible for fifty per cent of every relationship we are in. Our fifty per cent. When our relationships don't work we only ever try to change fifty per cent. The problem is we try to change the fifty per cent over which we have no control and no chance of changing. The other person's fifty per cent. If we want our relationships to change we need to change our fifty per cent. Systems theory ensures that the relationship will change.

This doesn't mean that the other person will be different. It does, however, mean they will relate to us differently. In a scenario I have seen played out many times, a wife who suspects her husband of being unfaithful tries to get him to change his behaviour. She asks questions, pesters and demands. The husband becomes defensive, remote and withdrawn. His behaviour stays the same or worsens.

Replayed using the heroic rule of relationship, the wife, who is sick of feeling insecure and alienated, decides she wants to feel alive and at peace with herself. While she wants her relationship to work, she shifts her focus to activities that give her pleasure. As her confidence and contentment grow, she radiates warmth and excitement. She invites her husband to share more of her world. He is intrigued, somewhat threatened, but drawn to get to know his wife better. She is more direct, more alive. She invites him to do things that rekindle the flame in the marriage. Slowly, he loses interest in all of his extramarital affairs. Alternatively, he doesn't respond to his wife's new outlook, so his wife leaves to get on with the exciting life she has created for herself.

In either case, by changing *her* 50 per cent, the wife has changed the relationship. The same principle applies in the workplace. Bring an alive, interesting and purposeful you to the office environment and you will be amazed at how much power you have.

Questions to ask yourself

1. How do you think it might benefit you to take responsibility for 50 per cent of every relationship that you are in?
2. Think of an issue you currently have with somebody who is part of your work or personal life. What needs do you have in this situation?
3. What are you doing to meet your own needs?
4. If we want our relationships to change then we need to change our 50 per cent of the relationship. What could you do to enhance this relationship?

Lessons for relationships

Agreeing on relationship rules up front simply makes life easier.

Sitting listening to a group of executives from large international companies discuss the do's and don'ts of client/supplier partnerships, I was amused that large companies have got it so right with these complicated relationships while they are struggling so sorely with ones closer to home. It seemed to me that there were three key lessons that the executives could teach themselves based on their experience with business partners.

Lesson 1: In relationships that matter it is essential to invest time and money.

One executive told us that his company spent up to $2 million on professional relationship facilitators for major projects. The cost was so high because of the huge amount of time involved. Facilitated negotiations began as much as six months before anything was signed. It was believed that the cost of facilitation was totally justified by the fact that a good partnership could save ten to twenty times the cost of facilitation, as well as minimise time lost later in disputes.

These executives had a model for building up understanding and goodwill before the problems began, and they had no qualms in seeking professional help to do this. I wondered how many executives transfer this learning to their personal lives – really investing in their relationships with life partners and seeking professional help without feeling that to do so showed some failure on their part.

Lesson 2: Choose your partners well

One of the executives related how he had recently let two multimillion-dollar contracts go because he believed that the hassles associated with the companies involved would be too time consuming and would sap his profit margins. I have heard this often from those committed to partnership marketing – they will walk out of early negotiations, fail to reply to tender invitations, and avoid rebidding for business if their would-be partners are too immature and unskilled in relationships to make a partnership work.

> **If we want our world to work then it matters that our relationships work.**

'How wonderful,' I thought, 'that these executives had the good sense not to think that everything would be okay once the contract was signed.' So often we think that we can change a person once we have their commitment. These executives had the sense to realise that robust, effective relationships are hard enough to achieve without the obstacle of trying to make them work with people who haven't the personal maturity or insight to even begin.

I again wondered if executives transferred this learning to staff recruitment, the selection of suppliers, and even to friends and associates. If we want our world to work then it matters that our relationships work. If we want our relationships to work we need to remember that we are only responsible for our 50 per cent and it makes sense to choose partners who are capable of taking responsibility for their half.

Lesson 3: Negotiate both a contract and a partnership agreement

Most leaders are well versed in the need for solid contracts and good legal support. Those who are committed to partnerships are also going the extra mile and negotiating the relationship rules accepted by all parties to make the contract work optimally. If the partnership breaks down (ie, if the rules don't work), all parties are still bound by the contract.

I like the idea of relationship rules. In any leadership group with which I work we agree on relationship rules up front. It simply makes life easier. Experts on the growing number of 'blended families' also advise having family 'relationship rules' to help clarify expectations and agree sanctions and group norms. Knowing what is acceptable within a given context really does make life easier.

I find it amusing that when the success of a relationship underpins the possibility of greatly increased profit, people have little trouble applying processes and ideas they reject in other parts of their lives. Maybe by getting the practice at work, executives will learn how to relate better wherever they go?

Questions to ask yourself

We can learn a lot from looking at what worked well and what didn't work well in past relationships. Think about a relationship you have been in that was unfulfilling and see what you can learn about it by using the three relationship lessons.

1. (*Lesson 1: In relationships that matter it is essential to invest time and money.*) Did you spend much quality time together in this relationship? Learning from this, how can you improve the quality of time you spend in your current relationships?
2. (*Lesson 2: Choose your partners well.*) Did you choose this partner well? If not, what did you learn that will help you choose partners better in the future?
3. (*Lesson 3: Negotiate both a contract and a partnership agreement.*) What expectations and relationship rules operated between you and your partner? Did you negotiate these before you went into the relationship? If you were to revisit this relationship, what expectations and rules would you negotiate now?

Partnership rather than confrontation

Building effective partnerships takes skill.

Joe was in the middle of negotiations with a major customer. His lieutenants had worked with the client's people to ascertain their requirements. They had jointly come up with specifications, delivery schedules and service agreements and they had reached tacit agreement about price and a payment timetable. Now, however, Joe had to sit down with his counterpart, the client's managing director, and finalise the agreement. He was concerned because he knew he had no room to move on price, and he had indications that pressure would be put on him to do so.

As it turned out, his fears were unfounded, but they brought up the complex issues involved in partnership agreements. Relationships based on cooperation, networking and joint interest bring with them a need for greatly increased skills in communication. In confrontation-based negotiations we keep our cards up our sleeves and reveal as little information as possible. We play a wily game of cat and mouse, always seeking out the other players' weaknesses and exploiting them for our own best interests. Relationship in these situations means giving the other guy enough of something that he wants, and we don't want, to keep him happy. We keep our guard up and ourselves separate. We expose only those parts of the truth that give us the upper hand.

In partnership relationships, however, a whole new set of parameters come into play. We are talking about ongoing commitments where both parties seek to cooperate for mutual interest. We are playing a game of joint problem-solving, of sharing resources and of uncovering thorny issues that are blocking each party from maximum return. This game requires us to honestly deal with difficulties as and when they arise, to admit to mistakes, and to care more about optimising the common good than about saving face and winning. At the same time, however, business is business, and each party is out to maximise its own profits.

This makes partnerships about as hard to manage as a good marriage, in which both parties seek to optimise their own needs while at the same time working to ensure the increased wellbeing of other family members.

> **In partnership relationships a whole new set of parameters comes into play.**

With divorce rates soaring, we know that good marriages aren't easy to run. As a society, our relationship and communication skills are remarkably bad. It may be harder, however, for people to ditch legally binding partnership contracts than to get a new spouse. This may provide a strong incentive for leaders to learn about the dauntingly hard 'soft' areas of human interaction with mutual payoffs at home and at work.

Questions to ask yourself

1. What do you think are the benefits and challenges in committing to work with others in an open and honest way to find solutions that meet both parties' interests?
2. Think of an issue you currently have with a colleague, friend or family member. What are your feelings and thoughts about this issue? Have you communicated this to the other person? How could you work together to find a mutual solution to this issue?

What to do when the boss visits

*What can be done with a boss whose very presence
has a disheartening effect on staff?*

It must be that time of year – so many of my clients have been asking lately about how to manage visiting brass. The common scenario is that my clients have been working to bring about major culture change, which involves getting people to relate more honestly, treat each other with respect and work together to achieve ambitious strategic targets. All goes well until the boss from head office arrives and behaves in ways that are totally inconsistent with the message my clients have been working so tirelessly to get across.

I remember working very hard with the employees of a grossly overstaffed department of one organisation. My brief, set by the department head, was to get people to realise that they weren't doing meaningful jobs and to reassess their priorities and options. We were successfully on course, people were beginning to feel good about moving on to new horizons, when we were visited for 30 demoralising minutes by the organisation's chief executive. During this time he told us that saving money and doing useful work didn't really matter to him. The organisation was just fine the way it was. As he left I had an image that someone had opened the door and poured cold water on everybody present.

Time and again people ask me how to stop such bosses from making site visits or how to overcome the disheartening effects of poorly executed 'royal tours'. This, of course, isn't easy. In organisations where power has traditionally been concentrated at the top, insensitive and reactionary bosses have been major stumbling blocks to successful change. However, successful outcomes can be achieved even in the most extreme situations.

The starting point is to realise how much power you have over a visiting chief. To begin with, if the boss is visiting you, he or she is on your ground. You and your people have him/her outnumbered and you are usually in the position to set the agenda. You can, if you choose, see the visit as a wonderful opportunity, not to get the boss's approval, but to educate him/her on your way of seeing things.

> ❝ **Insensitive and reactionary bosses have been major stumbling blocks to successful change.** ❞

I once worked with a group of people who were awaiting the arrival of the 'big boss' with trepidation. I was told that he never answered straight questions, always strayed from the agenda, came late and left early. I convinced these people to decide well in advance what they wanted from this 'dignitary'. They wrote out their objectives and then devised a plan for managing the boss when he arrived. Instead of just presenting what they had been doing and waiting for his comments, they prepared a list of questions, things on which they wanted his advice. They worked out ways of including him as a working member of their meeting.

The exalted figure arrived and the group swung into action behind their plan. When discussion strayed away from the objectives, group members took turns in bringing it back on course. Not only did the group meet all its objectives but the boss stayed so long they eventually asked him to leave so they could move on to other agenda items in which he was not involved.

So often we look at our organisational superiors as though we are children and they are adult authority figures. Instead of dealing with them sanely as we would with any other human being, we regress and act out of old subconscious patterns which greatly diminish our personal power and effectiveness. How surprised people seem to be when they realise that they can manage the boss by managing their own thinking, making bold choices and cooperating with their team members to achieve common objectives.

Questions to ask yourself

1. How do you deal with difficult people who are in a position of power? Is your strategy working?
2. What other strategies might you add to your repertoire? What parts of your current strategy might you change?
3. What strategies have you seen other people using that worked?
4. Often we try and deal with difficult people on our own rather than seeking support and help from others. From whom in your work environment could you seek support and help in managing difficult people?

Your boss needs praise too

How much better the world would be if we helped each other to grow and learn rather than sneer at other people's fumbling attempts to develop.

Australians love to pull down the tall poppy, support the underdog and see people levelled. Perhaps it comes from our convict heritage or the ruggedness of the Australian bush, or the heat. Whatever the reason, we, as a nation, don't like people who strive to raise themselves above the crowd. We like even less people who 'suck up' to people in authority.

John was talking to me about his boss: 'He reckons he's changing but I reckon he's the same as he always was.' A little later in the conversation John realised that his boss actually had changed in a number of positive and significant ways. 'Why don't you tell him?' I suggested. 'I'm no brownnose,' was the reply. How terribly sad. Having worked with John's boss for some time I knew that he was a man of great integrity, who was striving to modify his own leadership style so that he could empower his people to move to new heights both personally and professionally. The boss was struggling with these changes because they were so alien to the corporation's culture, and he felt exposed and unsupported. He craved feedback, some indication that what he was doing was worth the effort.

How much easier it is for us to stand back and take pot shots at someone who is striving to improve than to provide them with the dignity of human support. How much better the world would be if we helped each other to grow and learn rather than sneer at other people's fumbling attempts to develop. Perhaps we learn to conform to mediocrity in the playground where bullies set out to intimidate anyone who displays the vulnerability that comes with letting go of what we know in order to learn new ways of being. Or is it that if we support other people to grow, we too might be inspired to challenge our own sacred cows and ineffective habits?

> ❝ **How much easier it is for us to stand back and take pot shots at someone who is striving to improve than to provide them with the dignity of human support.** ❞

So often I have seen leaders pulled down by taunting, undermining subordinates who stood to benefit greatly by the leaders' successes. How much would it cost us to give credit where it is due, whether that be to a subordinate who is striving to achieve something of merit, or a colleague who is pioneering new ideas, or a boss who is striving to improve his or her leadership?

When I have worked with leadership teams and encouraged them to give and receive basic human respect, support and cooperation, I have seen the individuals in those teams soar to new heights, personally and professionally. Achieving a culture of support has never been easy. Giving and receiving human compassion, understanding and recognition is alien in most businesses – nobody wants to be seen as weak or sycophantic, and the corporate bully is alive and well. Still, when we manage to break through the barriers and establish a culture where human respect, honest feedback and credit is given where it is due, everybody benefits. Perhaps it is time to relook at our attitudes towards 'brownnosing'.

Questions to ask yourself

1. How do you feel and respond when others give you positive feedback – does positive feedback change your attitude and actions?
2. When you think of positive things about other people, do you let them know and, if not, what stops you? How can you overcome this resistance?
3. Think of something that somebody has done lately that has impressed you. Have you let them know?

When the boss is stressed

Hints for dealing with highly stressed bosses.

I was intrigued to read in a leading business publication an interview with a prominent business leader who, twelve months after the sale of his company, suffered from a series of panic attacks. He went on to describe his personal experience in adjusting to no longer being the head of a major international company. What was extraordinary about the interview isn't that a CEO had suffered a form of post-traumatic shock in response to corporate politics, or that he had trouble adjusting to retirement, but that he was prepared to admit it publicly.

The rate of panic attacks, high blood pressure, exhaustion, depression and other stress-related symptoms among leaders is high. What is low is their readiness to face up to their problems, either privately or publicly. One international high-flyer recently admitted that during a major international merger he was running fast just to stand still. He felt more stressed than at any other time in his career. His colleagues, however, appeared fine. Discouraged, he mentioned to a consultant, who was helping the company execute the merger, that everybody seemed to be coping very well with the stress. Not so, reported the consultant, who had interviewed all the players privately. Everybody was suffering from stress; it was just that nobody was admitting it. What this, of course, meant was that everybody not only felt stressed but, knowing only of their own stress, felt guilty that they appeared to be the only one having problems.

When people get stressed, they display some rather unattractive behaviours. They become easily confused, forgetful, negative and short-tempered. They often develop a crisis orientation, tunnel vision and seem to lose the capacity to think logically or creatively. Very often, truth and ethics suffer, as do self-awareness and self-management. So outbursts of anger, despondency and criticism are common. An employee who comes to a boss stressed with a problem can find this a very career-limiting move.

Another common symptom of stress is perfectionism. Stressed people make an art form of denial – they are just 'fine'. They have no problems. They are totally in control – just ask them. They might be a 'bit off' that day because of some external problem – the board, the market, the staff, the unions, the government, or the family – but otherwise they're just fine.

When the boss is stressed and in denial (the two go together), everybody suffers. Powerful stressed people share their stress around and create it wherever they go.

This means you could have a vested interest in helping your boss improve his or her lot. This is always a risky business. Telling people about their problems rarely works. While getting them to tell about their worries you can be much more effective, it bares its own risks. 'A problem shared,' so the saying goes, 'is a problem halved.' This is very true for stress.

When working with executive teams, we teach everybody the skills of empathic listening. This is the capacity to listen to the person behind the words. To listen to the emotional content of what the person opposite you is saying. When people are listened to empathetically they open up on an emotional level, get things off their chest and feel a lot better. The problem with doing this with the boss is that he or she can later feel very exposed and start to behave in a confusing manner, even rejecting the person who has helped them.

The chance of such rejection can be minimised by returning a confidence with a confidence – listening to the boss's issues and then sharing with the boss a time when you felt similar. Offering support can also minimise the chance of later rebuke. This, of course, can leave you exposed too, so you will have to walk a fine line. But then, if your boss is stressed, you will already be an expert at tiptoeing on eggshells.

> ❝ **When working with executive teams, we teach everybody the skills of empathic listening. This is the capacity to listen to the person behind the words.** ❞

My fascination is that we so readily accept stress as part of the job and so rarely question the huge economic downside of bosses who are unable to think clearly, face reality, manage their own wellbeing and relate in a sane and fair way. So often I hear leaders say they need help with their people but that they are okay. Such leaders completely overlook the reality that they themselves can have a huge negative impact on the working environment of their people and can create many of the problems that they then seek to fix.

Denied stress doesn't go away: it feeds off itself and infects the whole environment. I look forward to the day when stressed executives (in denial or not) are seen for what they are – workplace hazards – and are required to seek appropriate professional support services, thus making them safe to be around, a minimum requirement for effective leaders.

Questions to ask yourself

1. What benefits can you see in people giving each other support when they are stressed?
2. What type of support from others do you find most useful when you are stressed? Have you communicated this to the key people in your life?
3. What kind of support do you give others when they are stressed? Have you asked them if this is the kind of support they find most useful?
4. What do you do to support yourself when you are stressed? What else could you do?

three

CULTURE
AND POLITICS

Comfort zone

Happy to go with the flow? Not rock the boat?
Then maybe you're taking part in collusion for mediocrity.

In France and the US, books topping the bestseller lists question the intelligence and morals of US President George Bush. I can't say that he radiates an image of being the sharpest tool in the shed, but he is amazingly popular. So what is it that warms people to leaders who are most comfortable down on the ranch?

Recently I was talking with the chief executive officer of a large corporation about his forthcoming top-team workshop, which was aimed at inspiring his executives to engage in a period of rapid growth in quite tough conditions. When I asked what mattered most in the selection of a facilitator for the day, it became clear that comfort for the troops was top of the list.

Can we really prize emotional comfort above a job well done? Can we be happier with mediocre leaders than with leaders who inspire us to grow and be more? Unfortunately for most people, the answer is yes.

Emotional comfort is abetted by familiarity. We feel comfortable with what we know and will stick with it, even when it doesn't work. In discussions with a managing director recently, I was surprised to hear that he was retaining two big-name advisors whose work he had heavily criticised in the past. When I asked him why he didn't use a smaller, tested and more creative firm, he answered that the big-name firms were easier to get past the Board. Comfort versus effectiveness won again. The Board knew that the 'blue chip' head-hunters would come up with the usual suspects, avoiding uncomfortable change.

> ❝ **Can we be happier with mediocre leaders than with leaders who inspire us to grow and be more?** ❞

On the face of it this behaviour is quite bizarre. Surely people would want the most effective and wise leader running their country? Surely a managing director would want to employ people who get results (even if that means challenging people in new ways)? Surely boards would want to invest their money in the best talent? Sadly this is not the case. The psychological term for the reason is 'collusion'.

Collusion is the tendency of any group to cooperate on a subconscious level to maintain group and personal comfort. The rules of collusion ensure that we don't ask embarrassing questions, don't outshine each other and that we conform to the unstated group standard (or group norms). Collusion happens in marriages, friendships, businesses, community groups and on political stages. For example, if someone suspects that their spouse is having an affair but doesn't want to face the pain of knowing, they avoid asking questions and thus minimise disturbance of the status quo.

Hilary Clinton demonstrated collusion beautifully. Publicly, she apparently failed to notice Bill's behaviour, avoided asking the questions and kept the peace. Top teams and boards who fail to ask the embarrassing questions, thus maintaining the group's equilibrium and their own comfort, also demonstrate collusion. Those into collusion put around themselves advisors who keep to the rules, even if these people are poor performers. The problem, of course, is that when groups collude the problems stay hidden and are not resolved, so by the time issues do surface the marriage, company or country is facing a crisis.

This is what happened with Enron, WorldCom and Andersons in the US. The problems were there for all to see, but insiders colluded not to look, not to ask and not to address a reality that was bound to make people uncomfortable. It worked... in the short term.

Good relationships, good business and good politics demand that we face the truth and grow through it, regardless of the pain involved. Good leaders, particularly in times of change, are those who are courageous enough to challenge us to be and do more. This is rarely comfortable.

Questions to ask yourself

1. Think of a time when you witnessed or were part of collusion – at home or at work. What questions were you too afraid to ask? What truths were you frightened of that might surface? What made you choose comfort of the known over opportunities to grow and learn from the experience?
2. Now think of a time when you did challenge the status quo by asking the unaskable or speaking the truth. What did it cost you? What did you gain? If you were to do this again, how might you learn from your past experience? Might you gain more political support? Improve your communication skills? Learn more about managing conflict?
3. During which experience did you feel more alive – the one where you colluded or the one where you spoke your truth? Is aliveness and self-empowerment worth the risk?

Guilt-edged approach

Collusion can break an organisation's spirit.

With the bursting of the IT bubble and the crash of Enron and WorldCom, we were left wondering how problems could have got so bad before they became public. Having worked for over a decade with top teams and boards around the globe, I am more amazed that most companies manage to deliver a profit at all.

It isn't that leaders aren't intelligent, honest or highly trained. It's just that the human relationship dynamic in teams has a tendency to become horribly dysfunctional.

Over the years, I have asked members of the top teams of world-class companies which issues they avoided discussing. What follows is a summary of their answers:

- personal fears, disappointments and concerns
- people and their performance
- succession planning
- perceived business performance
- external business factors that seem to be beyond the group's control
- structure
- different accounting practices in the company
- profit

This tacit group agreement to keep key business issues off the agenda was studied by Janis Irving, who chronicled the group dynamics that led to a number of major military disasters –

including the Bay of Pigs fiasco (the site of a failed invasion attempt by anti-Castro Cuban forces, backed by the US, in 1961). What Irving discovered was that although individual members of decision-making groups knew that decisions being taken were wrong, they didn't dare voice their concerns for fear of exclusion from the group. He noticed that groups operating under what he called 'Group Think' had a number of characteristics. These included a 'them and us' focus along with a self-appointed 'mind guard' who pulled possible dissenters back into line. Desire for group acceptance was greater than people's fear of being involved in a catastrophe, even if they suspected the catastrophe would cost lives. This same dynamic has been chronicled by those studying industrial safety. Concerns about safety are often silenced through fear of being ridiculed or excluded.

> **The human relationship dynamic in teams has a tendency to become horribly dysfunctional.**

The pay-off is that everybody feels secure, avoids conflict and feels like they belong. The status quo is maintained. The downside is that problems don't surface until they reach crisis point, when they are far more difficult to solve.

Questions to ask yourself

1. Which issues/topics do you avoid discussing with your friends, family and colleagues?
2. What unspoken relationship rules operate between you and your friends, family and colleagues? Have you witnessed the 'Group Think' syndrome? Did you comply or speak your truth? Why?
3. What rules could you encourage in your relationships and any groups of which you are a member that promote healthy relating and honest disclosure?

Risking the easy life – telling the truth

It takes courage to risk the easy life by standing up for truth and integrity.

A 'half truth,' says the Yiddish proverb, 'is a whole lie.' This is disquietingly true. Recently there have been a spate of movies such as *The Insider* and *Erin Brockovich* that paint a picture of executives as liars. In *The Insider* – a tale of a high-level whistleblower in the tobacco industry – we are introduced to the Seven Dwarfs, CEOs of major tobacco companies that commit perjury to protect their right to produce 'devices for the delivery of nicotine', a substance they know to be lethal. In *Erin Brockovich* we learn that to save the cost of lining their waste-water ponds, the corporation PG&E (Pacific Gas and Electric Company) contaminate the local water supply and cause illness and death to hundreds of people. On discovering the impact of their actions, the company's executives go about lying and destroying the evidence in order to save their own hides and avoid expensive litigation. Erin Brockovich, through a combination of brains, memory, guts and cleavage, obtains justice for PG&E's victims. In *The Insider* the courage and anger of one man exposes the crimes of many.

Reflecting on both these movies, I realised how easy it is to see as villainous those executives who knowingly do the wrong thing. Yet many executives and professionals are implicit in unethical and even illegal behaviour but manage not to notice their own part in making the world a worse and more dangerous place. An unconscious conspiracy exists in most corporations and government departments. It is not so much about lying as not telling the truth.

❛ Half-truths add up to whole lies. ❜

In *The Insider* we see how whistleblowers stand to lose everything they value – their jobs, their families, their houses and their social standing. The more we have, the more we stand to lose. Somewhere deep inside we know that life is easier if we turn a blind eye, don't make a fuss or simply fail to notice things that are less than ethical, that represent less than ideal corporate citizenship. A vote for the half-truth is a vote for the easy life. In a world where the daily pressures of work and life are mounting, anything that makes our life easier has to be a good thing. Doesn't it?

As part of my work I encourage people to talk in 'I' statements. 'I' statements have three steps. Step one involves describing issues, events and problems without embellishment or judgment – a simple description of what actually happened. Step two is a statement of the speaker's emotional response to the issue, event or problem. Step three is what the speaker, not someone else, is going to do about the issue, event or problem or what they are going to do about their response to the situation. When people talk in 'I' statements, whole truths start being spoken. Thorny, uncomfortable and difficult questions start to be asked. Ethical issues are raised and discussed. Problems are quickly tabled and just as quickly resolved. In short, 'I' statements raise awareness, encourage humanity and empower ethical and productive action. What always amazes me is how much people hate 'I' statements, how resistant they are to use a tool that disables half-truths.

The problem is, half-truths add up to whole lies. Whole lies cause big problems. They even kill people. The questions, then, are: Do we have the moral fortitude to risk the easy life and tell the whole truth? Do we have the courage to be conscious of our actions and their consequences? Do we have the resolve to consciously choose actions of which we can be proud?

Questions to ask yourself

1. Think of a time when you turned a blind eye or simply 'failed to notice' activities that were unethical or problematic. How did you feel about yourself and your decision?
2. Think of a time when you spoke the truth and tabled a problem? What led you to do this? What did it cost you? What did you gain?
3. Are there currently any problems in your relationships or work life that you are trying to ignore? Fill in the 'I' statement form below about your reaction to these problems.

Step 1: When I think about

(objective description of problem)

Step 2: I feel

(your emotional response to the problem).

Step 3: What I'm going to do about it is

(what positive action you are personally going to take to deal with this problem).

Leaving bullies behind

Let's leave the bullies behind and move on to more successful, greener pastures without them.

Recently a client asked me to interview some of their consultants to see if they were compatible with my approach. The first interview was with a woman, a psychologist. She walked in and started abusing me. She didn't approve, she said, of any change in methodology that involved personal transformation for individuals. Such change, she claimed, was unethical because people didn't have a real choice as to whether or not they wanted to change.

Not long after this interview, I sat in on a top-team meeting. During the meeting, one of the men started to interrupt, talk over and abuse anyone, particularly women, who brought up issues he considered unimportant. Such issues included huge and potentially very expensive environmental issues facing the company, and concerns about staff induction. He was also very unhappy that people were asked for some personal reflection on what was probably the key strategic issue facing the company at that time. The man's behaviour infected the whole meeting – his aggression, put-downs and constant interruptions obviously upset people and slowed down both the meeting and the flow of honest communication.

I have often witnessed such behaviour as illustrated above. It is considered normal in business and rarely addressed; yet it has huge interpersonal, business and strategic implications. Such individuals create stress among their co-workers and employees.

They create diversions that freeze honest discussion of key issues. Their behaviour breaks down trust.

> ❝ **Effectiveness comes from operating at a much deeper, often unconscious, level that opens up the possibility of quantum leaps.** ❞

Some days later, I was in another meeting. In this meeting people felt safe to state their true opinions, including their fears, doubts and reservations. They took responsibility for their emotions, their communication and their relationships, and gave each other honest, responsibly phrased feedback. Over the course of the meeting you could feel the energy mount, the commitment lock in and the issues resolve. A huge strategic task was easily divided up and people willingly took responsibility for even the most difficult and unattractive tasks.

I was left wondering: what is it that so frightens people about creating effective, life-giving business environments? What is it that has intelligent people fight new ways forward that unleash energy, commitment, communication, relationship and strategic success? Why is it okay for people to bully, but unethical to ask people to look at their behaviour, take responsibility for the drivers that underlie that behaviour, and make personal decisions to work with those drivers and transform their behaviour and their relationships?

It seems to me that there is nothing more ethical than this. In the industrial era – the machine age – we fooled ourselves into believing that if you couldn't see and measure things, they didn't exist. Psychology became the study of things you could see and measure and we moved to a total focus on behaviours and competencies. We forgot about relationships, except for their behavioural manifestations.

Relationships are dynamic interactions on a physical, emotional and energetic level. They are more than a set of behaviours. For instance, sitting in a meeting you might feel that you have just been politically stabbed in the back. The feeling comes not from observation of a set of behaviours, but from 'vibes' that are generated through invisible, subtle but very real interactions.

As we move into the new, post-industrial era, effectiveness comes from operating, not just on the surface of things, but at a much deeper, often unconscious, level that opens up the possibility of quantum leaps. As we become more aware of this level and more skilful at operating within it, we gain competence in skill, power, insight and strategic success.

There will always be people who are frightened of the new. There will always be people who would rather stick to what they know, even if it doesn't work. The question is, will we let such people slow us down, or will we deal with them and their fear with compassion and progress to happier, more successful and greener pastures without them?

Questions to ask yourself

1. Do you have regular contact with anyone who acts in an aggressive, undermining and counterproductive manner?
2. What impact do such people have on you and your life?
3. What strategies do you use to progress with or without these people?
4. Is there a safe person in your life with whom you can talk about your feelings in relation to this issue?

Let's get rid of the bullies

Bullies need to be pulled into line so they don't
make life hell for those around them.

One of the unfortunate side-effects of the massive corporate restructuring of the past few years has been a rise in workplace abuse, with one in five people being a victim of punitive behaviour and language at any one time. Constant downsizing means that no job is secure, and sorrowfully this instability brings out the worst in those who are psychologically unfit. We know that tyrants undermine the effective running of autonomous teams, disempower others, destroy communication, and create an environment that induces stress, workplace accidents, time-consuming politics, and noncooperation.

From a psychotherapeutic standpoint, I know these despots suffer from stunted development due to painful experiences in childhood. From a management perspective, however, I know these people are a liability and only respond to strong, directive management from someone they see as more powerful than themselves. Basically, they need to be pulled into line and carefully monitored, or be removed from a position where they can adversely affect others. Like bullies in the schoolyard, they need to be removed and isolated to avoid making life hell for everyone else. This means that leaders need to be tough with tough guys for the good of the whole organisation. When they are not, everybody suffers.

Barry was the MD of a successful marketing company. He was a caring man who believed strongly in fairness, teamwork and mutual support. Tom, his director of finance, was a man who took pleasure in intellectual duelling and always being right.

Claiming he had no tolerance for fools, Tom treated most people, including Barry, with contempt, and put his huge intellect to use in order to prove how worthless other people were.

> ❝ **Why is it, when organisations are shedding people, that they don't take psychological health more fully into account, and do their best to get rid of the bullies?** ❞

The organisation, not surprisingly, was far from the strongest competitor in its industry. Barry responded to Tom's constant challenges by trying to avoid conflict at all costs, finding ways around Tom, and being nice. This freed Tom to strengthen his 'reign of terror' and to stage a well-planned and carefully executed 'coup'. Barry is now the MD of another company. His replacement quickly outplaced Tom and the company went on to substantially improve its performance.

Laws covering employment now make it extremely hard to dismiss anybody on the grounds of poor behaviour. When one of my clients repeatedly told me stories of how her boss undermined her in public, took away any assignment on which she was obviously performing well, changed the conditions of her contract without notice or discussion, and generally treated her with contempt, I made enquiries concerning remedies for the situation. Few came to light. The unions were aware of this boss's behaviour; government officials suggested she was oversensitive; and more highly placed managers within the same organisation preferred not to get involved.

These episodes certainly led me to wonder why it is, when organisations are shedding people, that they don't take psychological health more fully into account, and do their best to get rid of the bullies so that the healthy, capable people can get on with the job of making their organisations more successful.

Questions to ask yourself

1. Consider whether you have ever been bullied at work. What form did this bullying take and how did you deal with it?
2. What can you learn from this experience and how can you use what you learnt to protect yourself in the future?
3. Ask others if they have been bullied and how they coped. What can you learn from each other's experience, and how can you support each other around bullies in the future?

'Nice' guys don't need to give in to dinosaurs

If 'nice' guys refuse to play organisational politics,
they hand power to the people they don't like.

Have you ever wondered why 'nice' guys seem to fall by the wayside and their more ruthless colleagues push past them to the top? I did, so I began to take note of these instances. It seems that 'nice' guys make moral judgments about organisational politics and refuse to play them, while their 'less-nice' counterparts play politics to win. How often have I been told by a highly talented, intelligent and well-meaning 'nice' guy, 'If that's what I have to do to get to the top, I don't want to get there.' So they sit back being 'nice' and let their self-serving associates push pass them.

This gives the 'nice' guys license to complain about the way the world is being run and the conditions they, and others, have to bear. The game goes on and on. The 'nice' guys have got someone to blame for the things in their lives they don't like and the 'not-so-nice' guys get to rule the world. But who really is to blame? Is it the insensitive dinosaurs who push their way up the ladder or the lacklustre crew who forfeit their rights to improve their own lots, as well as their responsibilities for making positive contributions to their environment?

I reviewed recently the wins and losses I had witnessed in my career. What became very clear was that the losses occurred when 'nice' guys refused point blank to play politics. Instead they sacrificed their own peace of mind and the wellbeing of hundreds of people to the egos of ruthless and politically astute co-workers. In the three cases that sprang to mind, the 'nice' guys actually had the political advantage but they refused to use it. This led to two 'nice'-guy leaders resigning and another having to tolerate a highly inflammatory situation with an employee who continually undermined his authority.

> **Have you ever wondered why 'nice' guys seem to fall by the wayside and their more ruthless colleagues push past them to the top?**

In each case I had advised the 'nice' guys that they had to get the politics right. I had talked through with them the political steps they needed to take to protect themselves. In each case, my advice was considered totally unacceptable because it would have the 'nice' guys enacting behaviour that they associated with 'nasty' people. In other words, a means–ends inversion had to take place. Being more concerned with the means they lost sight of the objective, which was to maintain honest and productive work relationships for everybody.

The problem is that we affix moral judgments to certain behaviours because we associate them with people we don't like. Because we see self-serving egotists currying favour, we think networking and building relationships is politics and we don't want to play that game. When we see those we disrespect lobbying and building up the numbers to get their points of view accepted, we reject the technique instead of reframing it into working on our relationships one-on-one and giving people an opportunity to get used to ideas in private before they have to debate them in public.

Deep inside we know that in refusing to play the game we put ourselves at risk and let down the people who depend on us for sound leadership. By sticking to the high moral ground we are actually selling out to the dinosaurs who play for their own gain. To make our businesses, organisations and society the kinds of places we want for our children, we need to accept that leadership has very little to do with being 'nice' and a lot to do with tackling reality head on. This will include being 'tough' enough to deal with 'tough' guys.

Doing what you need to do to ensure that honesty, effectiveness and a fair go for all pervade may mean you have to get your hands dirty. Many peace-lovers have gone to war to ensure the freedom of their loved ones. In many cases being 'nice' is a cop-out – it is simply an excuse for not learning to be stronger, wiser and more skilful in how we handle our relationships personally and organisationally.

Questions to ask yourself

1. Do you let workplace bullies get their way by refusing to play the political games?
2. Think of someone you know who is an expert at organisational politics (don't exclude someone because you don't like them). What are some of the successful tactics that this person uses to get their own way? Taking all moral judgment out of their motives, what strategies can you learn from these people, and what can you apply to improving the common good and getting your job done well?
3. What judgments, fears and personal blocks stop you from being a skilful organisational politician, and what can you do to be more powerful in the workplace?

Laughable target for competition

Organisations willing to address and deal with the
'real problems' have a competitive edge.

'We want only people who are fanatics,' the head of one of Australia's top four warrior strategic consulting firms (let's call them Bonco Group) told Mary, their would-be marketing consultant. 'We don't want philosophers, people who are into working things through with people. We want people who will push things through.' Mary was one of my clients and she knew that she was being told that people at Bonco only wanted to work with warriors. Warriors are people who operate on the surface of issues. They deal in power, status and winning at all costs. Mary knew that this was an assignment where she would be expected to tell Bonco's clients what they wanted to hear.

This was going to be a problem. First, Mary's brief was to interview Bonco's clients. She knew that her skill as an interviewer meant she would be told the truth – something the folk at Bonco definitely didn't want to hear. Secondly, Mary is a woman of great integrity and intelligence – she wasn't into peddling lies for the sake of convenience.

As a halfway measure to ensure compatibility with her Bonco clients, Mary did a series of in-house interviews with Bonco staff. She found a group of people who were desperately unhappy and who failed to communicate honestly with themselves, each other and their clients. She found backstabbing, denial of reality and stresses that were preventing any kind of relationship marketing – any real marketing success at all. She decided to name the truth. Mary knew that this would probably mean dismissal, but somewhere inside her was a childhood dream that truth will win out, the good guy wins and doing the right thing leads to reward.

You guessed it – Mary was sacked. Bonco didn't want to fix up their problems. They wanted Mary to tell them how to stay the same and gain better results. They wanted some magic pill. We have Viagra® for impotence, Prozac® for depression, Disprin® for headache. Bonco wanted some painless, effortless cure for deep problems that lay in their own world view, their own relationships and their lack of relationship with reality.

> ❝ **The truth is, warriors will do just about anything to avoid facing the mess that is their own emotional reality and the state of their key relationships.** ❞

I was recently working with a new managing director who came into a company that had on its shelves over $20 million worth of reports from supposedly world-class strategic consulting firms. What was astonishing to the new MD was that although many of the recommendations in the reports made good sense, none of them had been effectively implemented. The theory was fine but it wasn't working in practice – something the high-powered, highly paid consultants had dismissed as they fronted up for yet another million-dollar contract. The hard work of dealing with the real problems that lay in the organisation's culture – lack of leadership and appalling relationships with stakeholders – was bypassed every time, wiped off as 'soft', 'not the real issue', and 'touchy feely'. The truth is, warriors will do just about anything to avoid facing the mess that is their own emotional reality and the state of their key relationships.

Now this is extremely good news for non-warriors – the people I call the heroes. When you look at the foolishness of the warriors, they become laughable targets for competition. The scope for gaining competitive advantage over people who refuse to face reality, refuse to deal with their own personal inadequacies and refuse to work on their relationships is immense. Mary has moved on to greener, happier and more lucrative pastures. The Bonco Group? Well, we'll wait and see.

Questions to ask yourself

1. Do you know any 'warriors' in your work or personal life (those who operate on the surface of issues and are mostly concerned with power, status and winning at all costs)?
2. What do you think is the downside of the warrior approach on a personal, organisational and global level?
3. What competitive advantages do you think non-warriors have?

four

PERSONAL DEVELOPMENT

Social denial of the unconscious

Our unconscious minds play an important role in our daily lives.

Adam Smith's 1776 book, *An Inquiry into the Nature and Causes of Wealth of Nations*, set in place a theoretical model for economic liberalism which underlines the ethos of capitalism. Central to this philosophy is the image of man as a rational economic being, choosing rationally between options under the invisible guidance of free-market pricing mechanisms of supply and demand.

One hundred years later, pioneer psychiatrists such as Richard Krafft-Ebing (and later, Sigmund Freud) identified the human unconscious – that part of our being which, hidden from rational thought, affects and interprets our conscious reality. The key drivers in the unconscious are in our personal, repressed, infantile history. We have all seen adults behaving like spoilt children who have failed to have their desires met. The corporate boardroom tantrum is a behavioural outpouring of the unconscious.

Extending the work of his mentor, Freud, Swiss psychoanalyst Carl Jung broadened the unconscious from the personal to the social level. Jung postulated that humankind has a deep interpersonal connection (the collective unconscious) that shapes how we perceive and deal with reality. Hegemony gives physical form to this theory. When I walk down the streets of Amsterdam or Sydney or Bangkok, I see look-alike shop signs – McDonalds®, Coca-Cola®, Jag®, Nike®. I see look-alike teens dressed in the current uniform of the young. When I go to a business meeting anywhere in the world, I see largely male groups dressed in look-alike business suits. While at a conscious level we might deny the collective unconscious, at a level of behaviour we live it out every day all over the world.

It is in the chasm between our belief in rational economic man and our denial of the unconscious (both personal and collective) that the rhetoric/reality disconnect is so firmly rooted. We base our business strategy and government policy on the theoretical models premised on the rational economic man. Yet it is real people (with all their conscious and unconscious complexity) who make the decisions and have to implement them.

❝ Most people are totally unconscious of their inner theatre. ❞

The most popular American writers (those whose voices have the greatest impact on leaders of business and government) seem to have studiously avoided any study of the unconscious and its impact on business and political behaviour, dynamics and outcomes. European writers (and, interestingly, US writers who choose to live in Europe) have managed to link the economic model of man with human reality. Notable among such experts is Professor Manfred Kets de Vries, head of human resource management at INSEAD. Manfred Kets de Vries (1993) writes lucidly in *Fools and Imposters* about the impact of the unconscious on leadership behaviour, thought and outcomes. He refers to our 'inner theatre' – the programming we bring with us from our genetic inheritance and early childhood experiences. It is through this inner theatre that we make sense of reality. It is this inner theatre that acts as the standard by which we judge what we see and decide what we want. It is this inner theatre that governs our actions.

Most people are totally unconscious of their inner theatre. Socially, we deny it exists. The collective unconscious of business sustains the myth that it is only what we know (that which is conscious) that matters, and all our decisions are those of rational economic man. So when we want to change behaviour, we study the behaviour and put in behaviour-modification programs. This is as sensible as trying to control the weather with air-conditioning. While air-conditioning can mollify the effects of weather, it does so within very limited confines and does nothing to prevent drought, cyclone or flood. Dealing with behaviour is about dealing with the symptoms, not the cause. It is about working with the tip of the iceberg, while sailing full-steam ahead into the hidden mass submerged beneath the surface.

The truth is that by denying the reality of the unconscious, refusing to make it conscious and work with it, we have institutionalised the chasm between reality and rhetoric. Leaders aren't necessarily lying when they say they are going to do this or that; they are just so unconscious of what drives them that they don't know themselves. This isn't to absolve them of responsibility but rather to say that as a society we are barking up the wrong tree. We have chosen to institutionalise a myth, and we are paying the price.

Savvy PR specialists, marketeers and spin-doctors have keenly honed skills of working with the unconscious (both personal and collective) without acknowledging (to themselves or anyone else) that that is what they are doing. Like the cunning of a street fighter, those who successfully manipulate the media are unconsciously tuned into what is needed to survive and thrive. Their lack of consciousness absolves them from having to reflect on the ethics and social consequences of their actions – a modus operandi sanctioned by social denial of the unconscious.

Questions to ask yourself

1. Think of someone with whom you live or work who has an obvious blind spot – something they cannot see about

themselves but is obvious to everyone else. How does this get in their way?

2. How could their life be improved by being more conscious of their behaviour?
3. Is it possible that you too have blind spots that are holding you back in some way?
4. Is there someone you trust who could give you constructive feedback to help raise your consciousness in this area?

Achieving, as opposed to winning

Trying to win at all costs is not a recipe for lasting happiness.

Julie is an outstanding woman. She has won awards for academic achievement, beauty and contribution to society. Bill, her husband, was extremely proud of her, but he was also extremely jealous. Julie, a high achiever, continually outshone him. She didn't mean to, she was simply rich in talent, spirit and goodwill. When I discovered that Bill was beating Julie I was shocked.

Bill was ambitious, he liked status and money, and Julie, with all her talent and charm, could help him achieve both. Bill's jealousy, however, continually got in the way. He saw other men ogling his wife and accused her of encouraging them. He saw Julie's growing success and found fault with little things she'd overlooked. As Julie's success grew, so did Bill's violence. Eventually Julie left. Some years later she remarried and became even more successful.

One day, when collecting the children from the harbourside home Julie had bought for herself and her new husband, Bill hissed, 'We could have had all this together.' 'No we couldn't,' replied Julie. 'Now I'm supported; when we were married, I had to fight you to achieve anything.'

**When we shift our focus from winning
to achieving, we empower ourselves.**

Although this true story (with names changed) is a domestic one, I see the same dynamic played out at work all the time. Some people just want to achieve. They use their talent and energy to get things done. They succeed and move forward, happily taking others with them. Their goal is to achieve, for themselves and others, whether that be their staff, their boss, their family or their community.

Other people want to win. They want to be top dog. For someone to win, someone else has to lose. For those who are highly competitive, achieving isn't enough, they have to beat others, to prove somehow that they are better – even, and this is the rub, if in doing so they fail to achieve. Bill lost. He lost his wife, full access to their children and the possibility to share the riches and joys a supported Julie produced. Bill wanted to win, to be top dog. His competitiveness defeated him. He got in his own way. Julie, on the other hand, was interested in achieving. When she couldn't, despite her best efforts, achieve with Bill, she moved on and achieved without him.

Elite sportspeople have learnt this lesson. While they want to win, they aim not to defeat others but to achieve their personal best. The only person they are really competing against is themselves. When we shift our focus from winning to achieving, we empower ourselves. When we focus on winning, our locus of control (where we place the power over our lives) is external, ie, we focus on people and events outside ourselves and gain our self-esteem from how we compare with others. This gives the external environment undue power over how we feel and react.

Achievers, however, have an internal locus of control. They are master or mistress of their own lives, emotions and reactions. They are their own people, seeking their own goals. They see others as allies in their endeavours to move forward, thus they achieve their goals with enhanced relationships and personal wellbeing. While sometimes this means achievers have temporary setbacks at the hands of their competitive colleagues, friends and partners, they wisely move on, their sense of achievement encouraging them to mix with like-minded others, get the job done, the project finished, the family built and have the group succeed.

Questions to ask yourself

1. Think of a goal that you are working towards. What motivates you to achieve this goal?
2. Do you want to achieve your personal best or to compete against others?
3. How could you motivate yourself in a more empowering manner?
4. Could you expand your goal in any way so that it will benefit those around you as much as yourself?

The perfectionist virus

*So many of us are now driven to attain 'perfection'. But what is
perfection, and is it doing us any good?*

I recently attended a lunch addressed by the 2002 Business
Woman of the Year. What an impressive woman! Having just
sold her multimillion-dollar veterinary pathology business, she
was working with the new owners to build their business. In her
spare time she is a scout leader, the mother of nine children and
is finishing her MBA.

The compere, a leading business man, introduced this woman
to the audience. He told us that she was the only person who had
ever made him feel inadequate. This feeling of inadequacy was
shared by several of my lunch companions. I found this curious.
This woman is extraordinary – she deserves to be admired – but
why do so many of us feel a need to compare ourselves with such
a role model?

While studying educational research recently, I came across a
social phenomenon known as the 'perfectionist virus'. If we catch
this virus, we choose arbitrary standards of perfection, then strive
to attain them. Of course, we never can – once we reach our goal
we raise our expectations.

**❝Perfectionists see the need for
improvement in everyone around them and
make overdemanding bosses and
judgmental co-workers.❞**

We all know that goals are great things. The problem with the perfectionist virus is that we strive so hard to be something we currently are not that we can destroy the very things that sane, healthy people value, such as health, key relationships and a sense of self.

Perfectionists easily lose sight of what is realistic and sensible. They have an overwhelming chance of becoming workaholics. Due to the psychological phenomenon of projection (whereby we see in others attributes and faults we are unable to accept in ourselves), perfectionists see the need for improvement in everyone around them and are overdemanding bosses and judgmental co-workers. Never being able to live up to their own standards, they are prone to depression, exhaustion and stress. In the education area, this is a huge problem, witnessed by a growing number of youth suicides.

I was speaking recently to an educated and erudite European businessman. He was reflecting on the American phase, 'What are you worth?' It took him a long time to understand that this phrase actually meant 'How much wealth do you have?' This way of looking at things was, until recently, quite alien to Europeans. Of course, the whole concept of being able to measure someone's worth is an offshoot of the perfectionist virus.

Perfectionism demands us all to be measured against some external standard. This denies and negates the intrinsic value and sacredness of our individuality. It also discourages us from celebrating uniqueness and diversity in one another. When we are constantly striving to be something other than ourselves, we fail to notice and value our uniqueness. This leads to depression, stress, misery and loss of self-esteem.

As an antidote to this, it's good to take time to listen to someone who you wouldn't normally see as a winner. I sometimes do this and notice that people who may not be young, beautiful, rich or powerful are often warm, kind and wise. They are often people who, when buffeted by life's trials, find deep within themselves a strength, a resilience and a compassion that they often use to make the world a better place. When talking to such people, I notice within myself the capacity to be more human. I notice how my imperfections are actually great assets, ones that are uniquely my own.

Questions to ask yourself

1. Part of being human is making mistakes. Think of a time when you made a mistake in your relationships or work life. Did you buy in to the 'perfectionist virus' and chastise yourself for not being perfect, or did you look at it as a learning opportunity?
2. Spend some time reviewing what you learnt or could learn from this mistake. How can you celebrate the learning that you wouldn't have received if you were perfect?

Maintaining our vitality

*We need to look after our health if we
are going to last the distance.*

'My hair's gone grey – that which hasn't fallen out – and I'm tired, physically and emotionally worn out,' James was telling me. He did look a lot older than his years. He'd been suffering from bad migraines, numbness in his limbs and back pains. He was also a self-made millionaire, having built up a small family company into one of the most successful, privately owned businesses in the country. A series of family feuds and tragedies had, however, taken their toll on his health and his emotional and spiritual wellbeing. He had great plans for taking the business further, even doubling its profits in the next few years, but he was worried whether his health would allow him to go the distance.

His story is familiar. 'I've never been more exhausted in my life,' the director of a major multinational told me the week before. 'The rate of change, the size of the issues and the complexity – I just never seem to stop, I'm hardly ever home, and when I am I just sit in front of the TV and veg out. All my colleagues and senior managers are in the same state, but nobody talks about it, nobody wants to own up in case they are seen as being weak.'

Both these men had done intensive leadership courses at leading institutions, such as Harvard, but issues of sustainable peak performance had never been discussed. It's almost as if, in business, the human being behind the role is immaterial, of no consequence. Seventy-hour weeks filled with constant activity, meeting demands and managing challenging issues and vexing relationships without time for reflection, renewal and self-sustenance can only lead to human wastage. This is of little concern to corporations that increasingly treat people as disposable goods. Those who wear out are simply replaced with newer, fitter versions. In many corporations you can't find anyone but board members who are over 50. This isn't age discrimination but sound business sense – if people have given all they have, they have little left to contribute.

> **People who nurture ongoing mental, physical, spiritual and emotional health have found the secret of sustainable peak performance.**

Increasingly we are told that we have to manage our own careers, not expect the mother corporation to look after us. We have to act as if we are our own bosses. In the one-person corporation we are all our own product, we sell our time, our ideas, our energy and our skills. It therefore makes great strategic sense to ensure that we spend a good deal of time on quality control and product maintenance. This means that a key factor of strategic success for any of us is that we ensure we are physically, emotionally, spiritually and mentally alive at all times. None of us would knowingly travel in an aeroplane that was not regularly serviced and well maintained, and yet most of us fly through life without investing sufficient time or energy into the key sources of our livelihood (our spirit, mind, emotions and body).

If walking in nature, night fishing or listening to music uplift your spirit, they are strategically vital activities – much more important for sustainable performance than spending that extra hour at the office. Likewise, working on your personal relationships with family and friends is an investment in your ongoing emotional wellbeing. We have all seen the fall in productivity that happens after a divorce, and yet we so rarely translate that into spending quality time with the people we love and working through issues to strengthen those relationships that support and nurture our humanity.

In my experience, the people who put the time into their ongoing mental and physical health and nurture their spiritual and emotional growth not only outperform the competition today, but continue doing so for longer. They have found the secret of sustainable peak performance.

Questions to ask yourself

1. Do you make time for reflection, renewal and self-sustenance in your life? What helps you do this?
2. Are you in good physical, emotional, mental and spiritual health? Are there any aspects of yourself that need more attention?
3. Make a list of the things that give you joy. When was the last time you did each of these things? Diarise these activities to ensure you spend more time doing the things that you enjoy.

Challenge yourself

*To go after what you truly want you need to step
outside of your comfort zone.*

I had been mentoring a client, Art, for several months. Then one morning he complained that we were moving too slowly. He was right, of course, we had been working at a snail's pace, helping him achieve some uninspiring goals. So I asked him what he really wanted. He drummed out some pedestrian objectives that seemed like a cop-out to me. He agreed that they were. So I kept asking him what he wanted until we got through all the objections, self-doubts and self-limiting beliefs to something that made his face light up.

Recently married, what Art really wanted was to own his own home within five years. That meant doubling his current income in the next two years. So we looked at how he could be worth twice as much to his employer in that period. Again he hedged around, using phrases such as, 'by supporting other managers', 'by planning for', and 'by being part of' – anything that avoided him actually taking personal responsibility for making a big impact on the bottom line. Eventually he ran out of time and excuses and decided he personally could be responsible for a 25 per cent increase in productivity and a 10 per cent increase in profit, within his work team.

**❝Change doesn't happen until
the desire for something new is
greater than the fear of change.❞**

Of course, this would mean taking some pretty big risks, sticking his neck out, learning to understand and skilfully manage the political system, and becoming hugely more strategic in his use of time and way of thinking. Still, the goal was worthwhile. He could see that work would become a lot more interesting. Moreover, with the changes taking place in his industry it was really a matter of 'grow or leave'.

Over the years, I have found that people will go on doing what they have always done until they commit to something of sufficient challenge and promise to have them overcome their personal inertia and move out of their comfort zone. It's almost as if change doesn't happen until the desire for something new is greater than the fear of change.

Of course, the negative side of this applies too: people change when fear of the known is greater than fear of the unknown. However, changes motivated by fear have a lot less energy in them than changes motivated by strong desire. When we are wanting to move out front as leaders, heartfelt dreams are stronger allies than fear. Sure, we'll baulk at things from time to time but, like the mountain climber, it is the desire to get to the top that will have us overcome obstacles and find solutions to problems.

This way of operating is exhilarating. Many of us hide in the supposed safety of conformity and familiarity – we think we will be protected by reacting to our environment, by not sticking our necks out or taking risks. Really wanting something puts us on the line. Once we commit to actually making a difference, to going after something that matters to us, we are compelled to grow and come to life in self-empowering ways.

Questions to ask yourself

1. What are your key goals for the next five years with regard to your work, your relationships, your health, your finances and your social life? Write them down.
2. Take a look at these goals. Are these goals what you truly want, or is there something greater that you want for yourself that you haven't dared to consider? Write down your expanded goals.
3. How are you going to make these goals happen?

Listening to the inner self

Worldly success does not necessarily lead to
inner happiness and contentment.

By the age of 40, Peter had achieved all his goals. He had set up a successful engineering company and he had a beautiful wife and three gorgeous kids. He owned his own house and was fit and healthy. He was far ahead of where his parents had been at the same age. In fact, he had achieved all his goals along with the hopes that his parents had had for him. So why wasn't he content? He had always been project-driven and he planned out a number of ongoing projects, but none of them really caught his imagination. Somehow the passion had gone.

I've had many 'Peters' come to see me over the years. They seek my help because they are at a turning point in their businesses. They want to train a replacement so they can move on to new things, or they want to restructure their company, or perhaps they are not getting on with certain members of their team. Often they are just ready to move on to the next stage of success. Whatever the reason, it is always about some issue they see as being external to themselves.

As we talk it becomes clear to me that their pursuit of success has been aimed at achieving happiness, fulfilment and peace. They wanted security for themselves and their families, some greater meaning to life, but they enjoyed the excitement of creating a career, a company and a success. They liked the social status of the power. To get to the top their focus had been on their goals and doing what was necessary to reach them. Once at the top, however, something just didn't feel right.

> **Without the appropriate state of mind no amount of money, prestige and power will lead to fulfilment.**

That, of course, is the issue. Happiness, fulfilment and peace are feelings. They are body-felt sensations that happen inside each of us. They can be momentarily stimulated by achievement, conquest or a pleasant experience, but lasting happiness, fulfilment and peace are a state of mind – an attitude that is internally driven. Without the appropriate state of mind no amount of money, prestige or power will lead to fulfilment.

Somehow society has been duped into a means–ends inversion. We seek worldly success so that we can be happy and content. However, in the very pursuit of success we often sell out our time with our family and friends, where we might develop our spiritual and emotional aliveness.

Over the years I have helped many people like Peter achieve increased worldly success by having them concentrate on reaching the internal goals of happiness, fulfilment and peace. By working on their relationships, clarifying their values and aligning their goals and behaviour behind an holistic vision of personal and professional wellbeing, they have moved forward both as individuals and as leaders.

In other words, they have gone out after what they really wanted – to be happy and to have peace of mind. They have found ways of running their lives and their businesses that supported those goals. The results in terms of personal wellbeing and financial rewards have been dazzling. As they move into new levels of success at work, they relate that they are spending more and better time with their children and their spouses. Their clients, partners, boards and subordinates are delighted by the changes. I smiled the other day when I received a call from someone I had never met. His message was simple, 'I don't know what you did to my boss, but thank you.'

Questions to ask yourself

1. What do you most value in your life in terms of work, family, health, friendships and finances?
2. Are you putting enough time and energy into these areas?
3. What could you do differently to ensure that you put your energy where your priorities are?

Gaining self-esteem from your being rather than your knowledge

The more you know the more you want to learn.

Before I started to work with you I felt more sure of myself,' Bill was complaining. 'Now I know I'm doing a better job, coping more with the complexity, but I feel more insecure.' Isn't it interesting that when we open ourselves up to new learning we begin to realise just how much we don't know? In my experience this is extremely uncomfortable. While we keep the blinkers on we can fool ourselves that we are in control. This gives us a kind of mock confidence and allows us to keep charging forward, unhindered by our own ignorance. While not knowing what we don't know might give us temporary assurance, it doesn't protect us from that gut-gnawing anxiety that maybe we are an impostor.

Working recently with a group of banking executives I discovered that most of the guys in the room felt that one day soon they were going to be found out. At a gut level each one knew that his or her pretence of omniscience was a highly fallible way forward.

Does this mean that we need to know everything there is to know? Hardly. It does, however, make humility an attractive option.

Have you ever noticed that the real experts in any field seem very aware of their ignorance? The more they know the more they realise there is to know. Accepting that we, as fallible human beings, can only have a lot to learn is simply facing reality. In a rapidly changing world this is the best protection we can possibly have, because it opens us up to learning on every level.

Facing the full extent of our ignorance can be very jarring and quite unsettling. In fact, it can threaten our entire self-image, especially if our self-image is based on our knowledge and expertise. If we rate ourselves in terms of what we know and we admit just how much we have to learn, we can feel pretty insignificant. For some people this can be so immobilising they close down to learning, change and personal growth. In today's world this is disastrous.

> **Accepting that we, as fallible human beings, can only have a lot to learn is simply facing reality.**

The alternative, of course, is to shift your self-esteem to who you are, to your being rather than your knowing. This is the shift to wisdom as against knowledge. Those in search of wisdom are always open to learning. They have what is called a beginner's mind – free of prejudice and open to new ideas, concepts and ways forward. Such people mature and ripen with age. They never become obsolete. In a time of knowledge explosion, those who seek wisdom are the ones who will make best use of the knowledge that is available. What's more, they will be comfortable with not knowing, and therefore with reality. These are the ongoing winners in our hyperkinetic world. They don't feel like frauds because they know it is all right to not know, to learn and to search for new knowledge. They do this because they feel good about themselves and pride themselves not on their static knowledge of today, but on the getting of wisdom.

Questions to ask yourself

1. What helps to build your self-esteem?
2. Are these things mainly superficial (what you know and do), or deeper (who you innately are)?
3. What are some of the qualities of your innate character that you value? (For example, creativity, the ability to build good relationships with others, the ability to see positive qualities in others.)

Some find compliments hard to take

When was the last time you celebrated one of your successes?

'When are you going to celebrate?' I asked Mark, who had just been tapped on the shoulder to head a US$1 billion business. 'There's nothing to celebrate yet,' he protested. I'd heard him say that before.

An Australian director of a major engineering company, Mark had first come to me when he had fallen foul of the politics in his division. Although he had performed well as an engineer and leader, he had managed to get some of the local players offside. I liked Mark a lot. He had great integrity, wonderful intuition and was obviously highly skilled in his craft. Like so many technically trained people, he hated politics and didn't play them well. Over the time we worked together, Mark realised that working on upward management of his international bosses and sideways management of his local peers was the one thing he could do for his people that they couldn't effectively do for themselves. This meant the relationships he had previously avoided became an increasingly important part of his job, allowing him to attract resources, along with technical and marketing support, to the projects for which he was responsible. More than that, he found out that not only was he very good at managing strategic relationships, he actually enjoyed doing so.

The projects that Mark oversaw rose in success and profile. He was then asked if he would be prepared to move to the US and widen his portfolio of responsibilities. This was about the third time along his journey that I had asked him when he was going to celebrate his success. Always, he told me it was too early.

> ❛ **What is it that has us raise the bar when we overcome our set goals, without stopping to enjoy the progress we have made?** ❜

Recently I was working with the senior managers of a large industrial plant. We were doing an exercise that involved the leaders giving each other positive feedback. I rated their overall performance as lousy. It was as if telling each other they had done a job well was going to choke them. The leaders seemed totally unskilled not only at giving the feedback but even at thinking up positive things to say. When I wanted to bring some public glory to these same leaders, they were reticent. What would people say if they let on just how well they were actually doing – how much improvement they had made, how successfully they were moving forward?

What is it that makes people resist celebrating reaching their goals? What is it that has us raise the bar when we overcome our set goals, without stopping to enjoy the progress we have made? For many there is a fear of self-aggrandisement: What will people think if I celebrate my own successes? For others there is a childish fear that it is somehow bad luck to notice their success. For many it is such low self-esteem that they don't think they are capable of anything worthwhile.

I have some clients for whom it is virtually impossible to accept a compliment. They are worried that they will become conceited – that they will somehow be weakened by acknowledging they have done something worthwhile. However, we all need positive reinforcement. The affirmation that comes from acknowledging a job well done gives the positive energy we need to begin the next challenge. Rather than weakening our chances of success, acknowledging our achievements helps carry us through the hardships that will be an inevitable part of our onward journey. Moreover, celebrating our achievements together helps build relationships. Sharing the good times helps us to work together when things aren't so good. Honest affirmation builds our self-esteem, which helps us to be more flexible in our thinking and braver in our risk-taking. People who feel good about themselves are better at relationships, decision making and achieving results.

Questions to ask yourself

1. Think about a time when you achieved something great and celebrated the success. What difference did the celebrating have on the way you felt?
2. Think about different ways that you could celebrate when you achieve a goal. What are they? For example, buying a special gift for yourself, having a nice dinner with a good friend, going on a holiday, treating yourself to a massage.
3. Think about a goal you have achieved recently or in the past. Can you celebrate it now?

The power of positive thinking

In order to achieve our true potential we need to adopt empowering beliefs.

Organisations around the world are embarking on programs aimed at attitude change. Unfortunately, most of these programs are based on a very shaky understanding of human personality. Our attitudes are based on our beliefs and our beliefs are generalisations based on painful and pleasurable experiences from our past. Some beliefs – such as, 'If I set my mind to it I can do anything' – are empowering, and others – such as, 'I'm too old to change', 'Women will always be stopped by the glass ceiling', or 'If you want something done well you have to do it yourself' – are disempowering.

Empowering beliefs enrich and enliven our world and contribute to our success and happiness. Disempowering beliefs paralyse us emotionally and intellectually and stop us achieving our potential in every area of our lives.

Although beliefs are emotionally based, they appear as intellectual constructs that shape the way we view the world. So subtle are these constructs that we come to think the world is as we believe it to be. So if we truly believe that we have to do everything ourselves, we actually delegate to people who let us down often enough to prove our beliefs right. This may happen because we 'forgot' to give them enough information or power or support, or because we delegate to the wrong people. Conversely, if we believe we will succeed, there is a higher-than-likely chance that we will. Dr Martin Seligman in *Learned Optimism* studied salesmen in the insurance industry and found that optimism was the greatest predictor for success. Those who believed they would succeed, did – independent of tested ability.

If some beliefs help and some don't, it is worthwhile reinforcing the empowering beliefs and changing the disempowering ones. The easiest way I know to do this is to listen to and write down self-talk. Simply take notice of and chronicle that small voice running inside your head that tells you what you are doing wrong, how you could do things better and what others think about you. Then you need to go through the process of deciding which of your beliefs are helping you and which you would like to change.

> **If we believe we will succeed, there is a higher-than-likely chance that we will.**

For those beliefs you wish to change, simply write down the disempowering ones on a sheet of paper. On another sheet write down the empowering beliefs you would like to adopt. If you believe you have to do everything yourself, you could choose to replace this with a belief that says, 'I easily select the vital things I need to do myself and successfully delegate other tasks/projects to the competent people around me.' Now, it is likely that your immediate reaction to the empowering beliefs you write down will be, 'What absolute rubbish.' This is because you are so strongly attached to your current belief system. So, for the moment, ignore your scepticism.

Once you have a list of empowering beliefs you would like to adopt, burn the disempowering beliefs and appropriately dispose of the ashes. Then read the empowering beliefs onto a tape and listen to the tape three times a day for ten weeks. You can listen to your tape while you are travelling to work, shaving, putting on your make-up or preparing for bed. Ten weeks seems to be the length of time necessary for a belief to change.

I have seen people save marriages, get promotions and give up smoking through using this technique. I use it to motivate myself to new levels of performance or to change negative mind-sets. Two years ago I remembered this technique, which I had forgotten for some years. I wrote down my beliefs, made my tape and listened to it three times daily. During the ninth week my teenage daughter made her own tape. When I asked her why, she said, 'Mummy, that tape of yours has made the whole family so happy I decided to have one of my own'. I'm unlikely to forget the technique again.

Questions to ask yourself

1. What empowering beliefs do you have? Write them down.
2. What disempowering beliefs do you have? Write them down and reframe them as empowering beliefs. Read these new empowering beliefs onto a tape and listen to them three times a day for ten weeks.
3. What are some other ways that you can reinforce your empowering beliefs?

Clarity in change

The way out of a revolving door is to bring your focus in, work out where you want to go and then follow your own course.

The demands on those of us in positions of management are immense. We have demands from our superiors, our clients, our shareholders and politicians. We have demands from suppliers, staff, colleagues and the press. We have further demands from our spouses, children, parents, siblings and friends. All of these demands tend to focus our minds and energies outside of ourselves. We spend our days thinking, feeling and acting in ways that relate to meeting, minimising and placating these external pressures. Is it any wonder that at the end of the day/week/year we are tired, stressed and even physically ill?

Now add to this picture the increasing occurrence of change. We have change in technology, market structure and personnel. We have further change brought about by redundancy, marriage, divorce, birth and death of loved ones, illness, relocation and the general kaleidoscope of life. Our focus is, therefore, not only external, but changing. It's a bit like being locked in the middle of a revolving door. You very quickly get giddy. If you are looking out, and out is moving quickly, you become disoriented, confused and you often lose your balance.

The way to regain composure, to feel more in control and to make the situation work for you, is to shift your focus from the outside to the inside. The way out of the revolving door is to bring your focus in, work out where you want to go and then follow your own course. The door might still be spinning, but you aren't. An interesting thing here is that the door hasn't changed a bit – you, however, are no longer affected by it.

> **Most of us don't achieve because we allow our own negative thoughts and psychological blocks to get in our way.**

It's the same with management. If you shift your focus from outside, from the external demands and pressures, to within, to your own strengths, weaknesses, insights and capabilities, you can more masterfully deal with every situation that arises in the workplace. I'm not suggesting here that you cease to notice your environment and the people in it. On the contrary, as your focus shifts inward you will be more aware of people and situations around you. The difference is that you will feel powerful enough to take control of the situation rather than be subject to its wiles.

How to do it

Know who you are and what you want
The first step is to become more in tune with yourself. There are numerous books available that provide exercises in goal setting and determining your personal strengths and weaknesses – for example, *Wishcraft: How to get what you really want* (Sher et al.) and *Dynamic Laws of Prosperity* (Ponder). Go out and buy one. Do the exercises. This is your life; it is in essence all you have. Isn't that worth a small investment of time and effort?

Expand your awareness
Most of us don't achieve because we allow our own negative thoughts and psychological blocks to get in our way. The biggest problem here is that we don't even know that we are doing it. Your current view of yourself will be as accurate as your ability to see clearly and to be honest with yourself. Most of us have had little practice at doing this and don't see ourselves clearly at all.

Meditation is a good way to start raising your personal awareness, or try spending some time each day sitting still, concentrating on your breath or focusing on a flower, a tree or a picture. If your mind wanders, just notice that this is what happens and bring your attention back to your breath or the object. This exercise is simply stilling your mind enough to notice.

Bring the centre of power in

Once you have worked out who you are, what you want and have started to notice how you really operate in the world, you may have begun to see that the problem isn't 'them' or 'life' or 'work' or 'children', it's the way you deal with them. Life and people go on being who they are – you can't really change that. You can, however, change how that affects you. You are half of every relationship that you have. If you change your half, you change the relationship.

If you are being used by people, learn how to say 'no' – read *How To Say No Without Feeling Guilty* (Breitman et al.) or take a course in assertiveness training. If you are constantly being rejected by others, notice how you feel about yourself and notice how you act when you feel unlovable. Maybe you are rejecting them, or making it impossible for them to do anything but reject you. Maybe you are also picking the wrong people – read *Women Who Love Too Much* (Norwood).

Vote with your feet

Petrea King, counsellor, writer, public speaker and 'midwife' to those dying with AIDS and cancer, told me recently, 'Dying is terrific because you live every single day as if it is your last.' Do you? If you are exhausted because you are bogged down just staying alive, stop. If you were going to die tomorrow, next week, next year, what would you be doing today? Well, you weren't put on the planet with a guarantee that you would be alive tomorrow. So stop doing the things that get you down and do the things that you want to do.

Embrace the truth (good and bad)

This may mean facing up to a few home truths. Are your relationships working? Are you challenged and fulfilled in your work? Are you getting the rest, relaxation and spiritual peace that you need? If not, what are you going to do about it? You can deny, ignore and avoid reality forever, being only half alive, or you can decide to live, starting today, and take the risk of being yourself, stating your needs and living your life your way. Only you can decide.

Develop your relationships

You don't have to do this alone. In fact, ensuring you have in your life a group of caring and supportive friends is invaluable. As you change you will probably feel resistance from your family and friends. They were used to you the way you were and will probably find it uncomfortable to learn new ways of relating to you. However, as you become more self-aware and more personally powerful you will also become more attractive to others. The truth is that some of your existing relationships will fall away and others will start up. The endless tide of birth, maturity and death applies to all living relationships. Welcome the pain and the joy of change and learn from it – this is life you are experiencing.

Questions to ask yourself

1. What external demands and pressures do you have in your life?
2. What strengths do you have that help you to cope with these pressures?
3. What can you do to reinforce these strengths?

five

LEADERSHIP

Directions

Leaders in the 21st century will need to think in entirely new ways.

There was a time when everybody thought that the world was flat. Yet people could see that when ships appeared in the distance, you could see the mast first. This didn't make sense if the world is flat. But people were so committed to their belief that the world was flat that they preferred to discredit what they saw with their own eyes. More than that, they were prepared to punish anyone who challenged the popular beliefs of the time, even if that person was right. So people such as Copernicus and Galileo were condemned and even locked up for demonstrating that the Earth rotated around the sun, not the other way around. Eventually, though, over quite a long period of time, it came to be accepted (by most, anyway) that the world was round and that it rotated around the sun. The old mind-set became outdated and what was once heresy became common sense. The paradigm had shifted.

> **We need innovative and visionary leaders with the ability to create a new world view.**

Is there a parallel here with much of today's top management? Consider the following:

- A Booze Allen Hamilton survey showed that CEO turnover at major corporations increased by 53 per cent between 1995 and 2001 (see www.ceogo.com), and L. Cambron in *Far Eastern Economic Review* states that from 1997 to 2002, close to two-thirds of all major companies replaced their CEOs.

- Warren Bennis and James O'Toole report that boards repeatedly hire the wrong CEOs because board members don't understand what good leadership is or how incredibly effective it can be in developing exceptional organisations. Through their actions in dismissing underperforming CEOs, boards live out their intuitive knowledge; but when it comes to choosing a replacement they operate via quite a different agenda.

The fact is that most people at the top end of business were reared with a mind-set that actually limits their comprehension of what they see with their own eyes. Board members are firmly rooted in an outdated mind-set. Metaphorically, most of them still believe that the earth is flat.

The new world view

Charles Handy in *Beyond Certainty* tells us that we are in a time of discontinuous change. This simply means that we aren't changing along a continuum, but are actually moving into a whole new paradigm. Discontinuous change is resulting from an accumulation of things, including:

- globalisation and the increased competition it brings
- globalisation and the adverse reactions it creates, e.g. protests in Seattle, Davos and Prague against the World Trade Organization and the World Economic Forum
- the increasing concentration of wealth – both private wealth and corporate wealth
- technological change, particularly information technology and the internet

- changing social values, especially about environmental issues, corporate citizenship and ethics
- the movement from the industrial era to the information/ services era (services account for more than half of the GDP of developed countries and is the fastest growing component of the GDP).

Further, the rate of change is an exponential curve. In such a situation, doing the same thing harder, faster and more often is not going to make it the right thing to do. But doing the right thing speeds everything up and makes things more effective.

In 1996 I was asked to work with the European heads of manufacturing of BP Oil Europe as they merged their organisation with Mobil Oil Europe. This was a merger of some 17 000 people valued at around US$5 billion. We had six months to implement the merger. At the time, BP Oil Europe had been the company's poorest-performing asset for years. One year later, the merger was bedded down and the merged company made a record profit, becoming the highest performing part of the company's European portfolio.

What worked? Four things:

1. The leaders adopted e-world thinking. They began to move to a holistic world view, looking at the relationships between things, rather than concentrating on the 'bits'. They concentrated on outputs, not inputs.
2. Each leader worked personally to build up their emotional and spiritual resilience and competence. This allowed them to get the right things done and commit to transforming themselves, their relationships and their parts of the organisation.
3. The leaders concentrated on relationships, relationships and relationships.
4. All of the above was applied to strategic reality. Learning was done around real strategic and human situations, and tested

against real strategic and human situations. The organisation became a real-time learning organisation.

Let's look at these four elements in more detail.

1. *E-world thinking*

About 300 years ago we were all getting excited about the invention of machines. Machines revolutionised our world. Factories were built to house machines and towns, then cities grew up around the factories. People left the land and came to the towns and cities to find work. This led to the breaking down of the extended family and the rise of urbanisation. As machines got more sophisticated, we needed a more educated workforce, so we saw the rise of mass education. As machines got smarter we saw the rise of mass higher education. Over time, the power of the landed gentry passed to the industrialists, merchants and bureaucrats.

But the industrial era did more than reshape the way we lived and worked. It also totally imbued the way we thought. The machine was the dominant analogy during the industrial era. We applied it to organisations (working to create well-oiled machines), to the human body (food became the fuel for the machine) and to social systems.

Based on principles of Newtonian physics, industrial-era thinking encouraged us to break everything down into its component parts: understand the parts and then reconstruct the whole.

We applied this to education itself. We didn't learn how to think, how to relate or how to make sense of reality. We learnt maths, science, English, history and geography as separate – and largely theoretical – bits. We weren't tested on our capacity to relate this learning to reality, but rather on our understanding of the inputs. We passed or failed exams on our capacity to learn the data and reiterate it.

Adam Smith, in his 1776 treatise on capitalism, captured the machine-age ethos. His belief that efficiency lay in specialisation and that this would form the basic dynamic of the economy became the dominant mind-set. The industrial era was the age of empiricism. If you couldn't see it, touch it and measure it, it didn't exist.

Newtonian physics taught us that if you set a train of events into operation on one occasion, and did the same again under the same set of conditions, you would get the same outcome. So one of the driving forces of the machine age has been the move to standardisation, and the necessity to control all the conditions to ensure standard results. This became the science of Total Quality Management.

Science was king during the industrial era – we saw the rise of scientific management and time-and-motion studies based on scientific management. We became so carried away with this theory that we extended it to everything, including the inner workings and relationships of human beings. It was the measurable, observable behaviours, such as skills and competencies of the human resources, that became the interest of the time-and-motion experts. We developed a whole science around it: psycheology. Through the study of the behavioural measurable activities of humans (and assorted animals – mainly monkeys and mice) under laboratory conditions, psychology provided guidelines for the control (euphemistically called management) of human resources.

Under stable conditions, or even conditions of moderate change, all this worked well enough. But under conditions of rapid discontinuous change, breaking things down into the bits, understanding the bits and putting the bits back together again is just too slow. With rising complexity there are too many bits. We can mitigate against some of this by breaking everything down into specialties, but then the relationships between the specialists become of paramount importance.

Trying to control all the variables under conditions of complex, rapid, discontinuous change is a fool's game (even Bill Gates can't control the internet). Anyway, with rapid change you may be working your butt off to control the old things that are now highly irrelevant. Under conditions of complexity and change, the game is to work out what matters or is going to matter next, rather than working out what used to matter.

With highly educated knowledge workers linked by the internet, the old practices of scientific management and human resources are breaking down. People want autonomy, authority, variety, learning and big dollars. If you don't provide these things, they move companies. When your knowledge workers walk out the door, so does the value of your company.

The rate of change, the complexity of the issues, and the uncertainty created by both of these, demand much more of everyone. We now have to develop more of our potential than just our behaviours, skills and competencies. Now we really have to work with our psyche. *The Oxford Dictionary* defines 'psyche' as spirit, mind and soul. While psychology purports to have been studying the psyche for some 100 years and claims that people are understandable and their behaviour controllable and measurable, the great religions of the world have been studying the human psyche for centuries. They all agree on one thing: the human psyche is immeasurable, unfathomable and mysterious.

Modern science challenges many of the basic premises of Newtonian physics. Chaos theory disputes the notion that you can recreate the same conditions again and again – even a small variance in conditions can lead to a major shift in the outcome. Systems theory tells us that all things operate in systems and all systems are interconnected – a small change in one part of a system can lead to a change in that system and to all the systems to which that system is connected. Quantum physics tells us that in the quantum world it isn't the bits that matter but the relationships between the bits. Nuclear physics shows us the immense energy in relationships.

In machine-age thinking the relationship is unseen, unmeasured and therefore considered irrelevant. In the e-world, relationship is all there is. The two worlds are compared below:

The machine-age world view	The e-world view – the emerging future
Industrial era	**Emotion, e-mail, e-commerce, energy, electricity**
Tangible, visible, measurable	Invisible, difficult to measure
Controllable	Difficult to control
Understandable by breaking down into bits	Heisenberg principle – complex and messy – the very act of studying something can change it
What you can see and understand is what matters	Relationship (the invisible fibre/space between the bits) is everything
People are cogs in the wheel of the machine	People are integral to, and drivers of, the system
Human emotion, soul and spirit are totally irrelevant	The human psyche (spirit, soul, mind) is central to relationship, creativity and co-creating your future

2. *Building emotional and spiritual intelligence (EQ and SQ)*

Adopting the e-world view encouraged the leaders in BP Oil Europe to go through a process of personal transformation to build their Emotional Intelligence (EQ) and Spiritual Intelligence (SQ) and, by doing so, to move from being ordinary leaders to being innovative or visionary leaders.

Warren Bennis (2000) defines leadership as:

...a combination of personal behaviours that allows an individual to enlist dedicated followers and create other leaders in the process. Great leaders demonstrate integrity, provide meaning, generate trust and communicate values – they challenge people and make them want to scale steep peaks.

Real leaders, in a phrase, move the human heart. But these, according to Howard Gardner in his *Leading Minds*, are only ordinary leaders. They do not seek to stretch the consciousness of the contemporary audience. They simply relate a traditional story effectively, thus engaging the hearts and minds of their followers.

In contrast, innovative leaders do all that ordinary leaders do, but also bring new attention to a fresh twist in the story. Here Gardner highlights leaders such as Margaret Thatcher and Charles de Gaulle, who, he claims, identified stories or themes that already existed in the culture and gave them a whole new lease of life. In refreshing an old theme in ways compatible with contemporary times, these innovative leaders have succeeded in reorienting their times.

But by far the rarest of leaders is the visionary leader. Not content to relate a current story or to reactivate an old one, visionary leaders create a whole new story, one not known to most individuals. Great religious leaders fall into this category: Confucius, Jesus, Buddha, Mohammed. And, on a more modest scale, we have Gandhi, Monet and Einstein.

Ordinary leaders need EQ. Innovative and visionary leaders need both EQ and SQ. Leaders with SQ have the ability to question, think creatively, change the rules and work effectively with new situations. This ability allows them to play with boundaries, break through obstacles, become innovators and devise new stories. In times of discontinuous change, motivating people's hearts and minds behind traditional stories is largely irrelevant. Getting people excited about being better machine-age players is a waste of time. Rather, we need innovative and visionary leaders with the ability to create a new world view and win the hearts and minds of followers who willingly engage in the uncomfortable but rewarding effort of personal, organisational and social transformation that will make us all winners in the new era.
But is even this enough?

Leadership is now a social function, with the appropriate person taking the reins at the appropriate time. In *A Brief*

History of Everything (1996), Ken Wilber provides us with a multidimensional model of leadership, which I have adapted for a business audience:

	INDIVIDUAL		
I N T E R I O R	**Intentional** (inner aspects of leadership – EQ & SQ)	**Behavioural** (observable and measurable leadership style)	**E X T E R I O R**
	Cultural (organisational culture)	**Social** (roles and functions)	
	COLLECTIVE		

In times of discontinuous change, the wider culture – affected by innovation, globalisation, changing values and pressing social issues – is changing. This changes the social environment in which institutions operate. The changed social and cultural environment now demands different behaviours from leaders, who then seek to work on their own EQ and SQ to cope with the changes. If they do this well they become good ordinary leaders.

For visionary leaders, the process works the other way around. Visionary leaders, through dint of character and judgment, notice that times are changing. They seek not to cope with that change, but to lead it. They seek to be part of the emerging tomorrow, not the dying yesterday. So they work with the cultural and social reality of their world, making sense of it for themselves and for others.

Visionary leaders have made working on themselves, intentionally and behaviourally, their life's work. They are self-made people. In today's world, Nelson Mandela is such a leader, as is the Dalai Lama. Nelson Mandela led a whole nation to a new possibility. The Dalai Lama is doing the same. Through bringing new meanings to a chaotic world, working on their own being and encouraging their followers to become more, to grow themselves as leaders, these two visionary leaders are bringing about global change.

Business, sadly, lags far behind. I have, however, in my work been privileged to work with leaders who have worked tirelessly to stretch past the ordinary and become more innovative and visionary.

3. *Relationship versus collusion*

We have recently experienced a global mergers and acquisition boom which peaked in 2000, with global mergers and acquisitions exceeding $3.48 trillion (it has since halved). A newsletter of Britain's Chairmen's Club (an organisation whose members include at least 30 chairmen from Britain's top 50 companies) identified the following cultural bear traps of merging corporations:

- incompatible time frames
- different value systems
- different attitudes flowing from being either a high-gross-margin or a low-gross-margin company
- different mentalities about capital requirements
- different error tolerance
- conflicting attitudes to work or ideas
- different organisational approaches
- different perceptions of whether a deal is a merger or an acquisition
- different ideas of customer service.

The impact of these bear traps is so great that the newsletter suggests the costs of mergers far exceeds their potential benefit. This point is not new. A recent Boston Consulting Group study found that 57 to 70 per cent of takeover bids were likely to destroy shareholder value for the acquiring company. If mergers are increasing, and incompatible cultures are the thing most likely to make them fail, then we need to understand more about culture.

Culture is the collection of social mores, or the 'on-the-ground result' of the unwritten rules through which people unconsciously agree to relate. To be part of any culture, you have to accept and act out the group's mores. When this is done unconsciously it is called collusion. Collusion underlies group think. Group think is the tendency of any group to protect its mores though mind guards. Unofficial guardians of the cultures will disallow dissent, objective discussion and even the tabling of significant problems.

Collusion in cultures brings about stability. In times of rapid change, the stability of collusion is likely to be looking to times in the past. That is a retroactive force, a force operating against tabling and dealing with things as they change, a force against building robust change-worthy relationships, a force against transformation and creativity into a newly unfolding future.

CEOs who want to turn organisations around have to turn cultures around. This is the work of innovative and visionary leaders. Ordinary leaders are too unconscious and too attached to old stories to even see the cultural issues and reality, let alone have the skills to do anything about transforming them. Ordinary leaders can tinker around the edges of cultures; it takes an innovative or visionary leader to transform old cultures into new ones. To do this they need high IQ, EQ and SQ.

4. Strategic leadership

But there is one further step to being the kind of CEO who can turn a company around quickly. Not only do they need to be able to build their own and other people's EQ and SQ, to transform mind-sets and win people's hearts and minds behind a new story, they also need to ensure that this new story becomes an 'on-the-ground' reality. That is, they need to ensure that what they say they are going to do, they do.

To do this, they need to have their whole organisations build EQ and SQ using reality. Most programs to build EQ and SQ are done in training capsules – detached from the reality of the business. Machine-age thinking had us scurrying off to training courses on how to influence people and control reality. All of this is out of date and way too slow.

E-world thinking compels us to do our emotional and spiritual growing, not in theory or in the splendid isolation of a classroom, but on the job, in relationship to the people with whom we work and the strategy of the business in which we operate. Remember, the energy is in the relationships.

Mintzberg, in *The Rise and Fall of Strategic Planning*, tells us that strategy has five Ps: plan perspective, pattern, ploy and position. Four of these five Ps relate to what we actually do. They are what Mintzberg calls emergent strategy – strategy that actually emerges as a consequence of our actions and relationships, strategy that is best seen looking back. This is the strategy that we live, the one that we actually implement, rather than the one we write in the plan that we are going to implement.

Thus strategy is actually the sum total of our individual performances (EQ and SQ), our actions and our relationships. Strategy is real. It is the thing that makes up the performance of our organisations. It is strategy that determines our share price.

As strategy is real, it is best to develop it using reality. This means that EQ, SQ and relationships have to be determined in accordance with strategy. This means that leadership and work teams have to get together regularly and work together on their personal transformation, in relationship to their peers and their business. Now this is a challenging thing to do. It is, however, what I have been doing with top teams for about fifteen years now, and it works.

Questions to ask yourself

1. Take another look at the machine-age/e-world diagram in this article. Would you describe your current world view as more machine age or e-world?
2. What parts of the e-world view do you think might be beneficial for you to integrate into your current world view? Why?
3. What changes might this make to the way you approach your relationships?

The long and the short of it

*In business as in life, a short-term approach makes
for long-term problems.*

A colleague of mine recently completed a course on assessing
the leadership competence of top teams. The theory of the
course, based on years of psychological research, rested on the
concept of:

stimulus + thought = response

Sensibly, my colleague pointed out that the quality of the thought
(and thus the strategic effectiveness of the response) rested on
a number of variables, including emotional intelligence and
psychological patterns of reaction, which have their foundations
in early childhood experience.

The logical outcome of this reasoning is that working through
self-limiting childhood patterns of thought and emotional
reactions, and raising emotional intelligence, increases the
'quality' of the thought and therefore the strategic appropriateness
of response. The problem I have with this is that I don't see leaders
thinking at all any more. They don't have time. What I see is knee-
jerk reaction followed by knee-jerk reaction. I see people working
longer and longer (decreasingly effective) hours. The long-range
focus of managers seems to have shortened to the state of their
company's share price over the next one to two months.

I recently went out to talk to a range of stockbrokers, investment
analysts and leaders of peak industry bodies to feel the pulse of

business. I wanted to know who was working to improve the future by making sound strategic investments. The feedback was pretty disconcerting. My informants (all people whose success depends on keeping a close eye on the strategic performance of major corporations) told me that, by and large, the top-tier companies were led by people who weren't interested in the future. The very best leaders had a time frame of three years; the worst had a policy of short-term self-interest. It seems that short-term self-interest is the order of the day.

We have seen disturbing examples recently of corporate mismanagement – Enron, Worldcom and Andersons – yet we manage to think of these as aberrations. The bestselling book *Rich Dad, Poor Dad* (Kiyosaki et al.) suggests that we should all strive to get rich at whoever's expense while doing everything we can to avoid investing back into the community. I recently addressed a conference for an organisation that represents volunteers. In the audience were people who head major community service organisations. I found them beaten down, demoralised and exhausted by the burden of doing the right thing in a society that values takers above givers.

> **❝I don't see leaders thinking at all any more. They don't have time. What I see is knee-jerk reaction followed by knee-jerk reaction.❞**

I also joined a group of company directors recently, and amongst other topics we discussed the rise of youth militancy – the riots in Gothenburg, Prague and Seattle. I mentioned how, when I was discussing with my husband our attendance at the forthcoming World Economic Summit, our daughter went white. She had planned to be among the demonstrators! There was a look of relief as I told this story, because it appeared that many of those around the table had had similar experiences with their children.

It turns out that while the young people in the streets may include some 'professional anarchists', there is also a large percentage who are highly intelligent, well educated and caring –

young people who see the self-interest of the leaders but don't know what to do about it. My fear is that instead of listening to the young and cleaning up our act, we will brand them as terrorists and bring out the riot squads, giving us older folk permission to maintain our stance of short-term self-interest. When you think of the long-term repercussions of such a stance, it seems obvious that the young will be in the streets. They will inherit the mess we are creating.

Questions to ask yourself

1. What kind of long-term future would you like for our global society?
2. How are you contributing to the development of such a future?
3. Is there anything else that you could do?

Competencies and character

Good leadership training focuses on the
development of character and judgment.

Our multibillion-dollar education and training industry stands in the way of real corporate development. We have defined 'skills and competencies' based on how superior performers have acted in the past, and we use this knowledge to define jobs, performance, training needs and levels of remuneration. A vast international industry exists to ensure that schools and universities train the young to meet this standard, while businesses and bureaucracies train, control and reward us for doing so.

Unfortunately, this standard is based on what worked yesterday. In fact, it is founded on a (mostly unconscious) theoretical model that underpinned the industrial era. In a time of rapid change this is both ludicrous and highly detrimental to individuals, businesses and the development of creative leadership.

I recently addressed a group of 'high-potential leaders' from a major IT company who had just finished a year-long leadership program. They were being trained to demonstrate 43 competencies. The possibility for subjective interpretation of each competency was immense, but the message was that there were clearly expected ways of operating, thinking and even emotionally reacting. These potential future leaders were expected, for example, to 'convey positive energy that captures people's commitment and stimulates creativity'. I thought about the world-class computer nerd, the guy who just might come up with the next multibillion-dollar invention. He is likely to be highly introverted and technically obsessed. While creative himself, he might display his enthusiasm by disappearing with his laptop for months on end. But our computer boffin was expected to be present and accounted for, showing 'enthusiasm, passion and energy, demonstrating cross-cultural awareness', 'coaching others, including peers, to achieve their full potential,' and 'using externally focused measures to monitor performance'.

'I've never seen anyone derailed from top leadership positions because of a lack of technical competence or conceptual skills,' leadership guru Warren Bennis has written.

'It's *always* because of lapses of judgment and questions of character. Judgment and character tend to be ignored by those responsible for educating others and are arguably difficult or even impossible to teach.'

> **❝Real leaders ask questions,
> take off in new directions and rock the
> boat. Real leaders are very hard to control.❞**

How often have I fought with clients who wanted me to teach them skills they had demonstrated admirably on certain occasions but had consistently failed to use on others? It wasn't lack of skill that had been their problem, rather a pattern of psychological reactions that prevented them from doing exactly what they knew was right. Managing conflict is a great example. You can teach conflict-resolution skills, but if people have an inbuilt terror of conflict (developed in childhood), they will avoid conflict until they have dealt with their unconscious programming – their 'judgment' and 'character'.

Character and judgment are developed by combining life experience with an awareness of, and freedom from, limiting psychological patterns. They demand awareness of the forces of hegemony that form the unconscious framework of our social and political interaction. We cannot be trained in this, so it is largely ignored.

Unfortunately, the old guard supports this sorry state of affairs. Real leaders, having developed character and judgment, tend to be switched on, creative, self-determining and empowered. Real leaders are in touch with their own unique talents. Such people don't fit comfortably into repressive corporate or government hierarchies; they ask questions, take off in new directions and rock the boat. Real leadership may hold the key to improved strategic performance, adaptation to the environment as it changes, and technological breakthrough – but real leaders are very hard to control.

Most organisations still operate on machine-age principles, where people are just cogs in the wheel of production, just one more input, such as finance, equipment or supplies. The aim is to maximise return on investment (ROI) in people while keeping them under control. When profit maximisation conflicts with control, it is control that takes precedence. Hence, organisations seek managers who can 'plan, organise and control' rather than leaders who can find new, innovative ways forward, inspire people to new heights and create the kind of self-organising systems that a rapidly changing environment demands.

Skills and competencies have a place, but when they become the main game they are killers. Training in skills and competencies focuses on externally defined and increasingly out-of-date standards. It robs energy and time from development of the innate gifts that people might bring to the task of finding new ways forward – evolving and adapting to the world as it changes.

Questions to ask yourself

1. What do you believe are your unique gifts?
2. How can you use your gifts to add value in your workplace?
3. If you are being forced into a corporate or social mould, what strategies could you use to create receptiveness for your gifts?

Leading your own life

Being a leader means taking responsibility for your own needs.

What is fulfilment and what does it have to do with leadership? These were the questions going around the lunch table. People were discussing their successes and their own journeys of growth. They were already successful leaders. Yet they had so many pressures in their lives that left them unsettled, unfulfilled and searching for answers.

I had difficulty understanding the problem. The solution seemed so easy. You clarify your values, simplify your life as a reflection of those values and put in place the support of people and practices that sustain you on your journey. This doesn't mean living in isolation on a mountain top or in an ashram. It means becoming the leader of your own life, dancing to your own tune, being what the Dalai Lama calls 'self-responsible' – knowing yourself, your own values and your own needs.

❝Becoming self-responsible is the key to powerful living, fulfilling relationships and real leadership.❞

The three most frequently asked questions here are:

- Isn't 'self-responsibility' just an excuse to be self-centred?
- Don't such people set themselves up for attack?
- How can we dance to our own tune when we are part of a society, go to work and belong to family groups?

It is true that self-responsible people are powerful and therefore often the target of criticism. We only have to look at great leaders, such as Christ, Mandela and Gandhi, to know that people who dare to be different, to live life on their own terms and to stand up to be counted, are very often a threat to those who would have us live lives of submissive misery. While becoming self-responsible carries risks, it is also the key to powerful living, fulfilling relationships and real leadership.

As mentioned, in *Approaching the Corporate Heart* I write about the 'Heroic Rule of Relationship'. This little-known rule of living, loving and leading is the key to self-responsibility. The heroic rule of relationship states that we are all responsible for 50 per cent of every relationship we are in. *Our* 50 per cent. When our relationships don't work, we only ever try to change 50 per cent. The problem is we try to change the 50 per cent over which we have no control and for which we bear no responsibility – the other person's 50 per cent. Systems theory tells us that if you change one part of a system, the system changes. Relationships are systems. Change your 50 per cent and your relationships will change.

It is our relationships – at home, at work, in the community – that appear to cause most of our problems. The heroic rule of relationship lets us know that our relationship problems come from wasting our time and effort working on the wrong 50 per cent. We have all been trained to concentrate on the other person. We spend our time trying to meet their needs, gain their approval, love and cooperation, and sometimes even their submission. When this doesn't work we try harder, doing more and more of the same thing, or we move away, reject, criticise and blame those who won't do as we wish.

A far more successful way forward is to change our own perception, be more strategic in our behaviour, clarify our goals and bring our communication, actions and intentions into line. All this requires getting to know who we are, what we want and what we stand for. It demands that we reflect on the messages we are sending – through our verbal and non-verbal communication. In the process we become self-responsible.

One of the big hooks here is that a lot of our behaviour, communication and relating are aimed at getting people to meet needs that we have not even admitted to ourselves. The unspoken agreement is that I will do X, Y or Z for you if you meet my needs for love, approval, success, recognition, power or status. If I have to tell you these needs then you have failed me.

Being self-responsible means acknowledging your own needs and finding appropriate, non-manipulative ways of relaying them to others or meeting them yourself. We then come to relationships as a whole person, seeking to share our life with others rather than using our relationships to fulfil us. Choosing self-responsibility allows you to be a powerful leader of your own life, to be in the driver's seat for making your relationships (and your life) work.

Questions to ask yourself

1. What are your current needs in terms of your relationships, your personal wellbeing, your work, and your time spent in the community?
2. How do you work to get others to meet these needs?
3. Is there a more honest, effective and self-responsible way that you can meet these needs?

Narcissistic leaders

Narcissists get ahead through self-promotion.

Psychoanalyst Michael Maccoby in his article 'Narcissistic Leaders: The Incredible Pros, the Inevitable Cons' (2000) suggests that those most likely to make their way to the top of large corporations these days are narcissists. He writes:

Today's CEOs – superstars such as Bill Gates, Andy Grove, Steve Jobs, Jeff Bezos and Jack Welch – hire their own publicists, write books, grant spontaneous interviews and actively promote their personal philosophies. Their faces adorn the covers of magazines like Business Week, Time *and the* Economist. *What's more the world's business personalities are increasingly seen as the makers and shapers of our public and personal agendas. They advise schools on what kids should learn and lawmakers on how to invest the public's money. We look to them for thoughts on everything from the future of e-commerce to hot places to vacation.*

In such an environment, those who are comfortable with self-promotion, who enjoy the spotlight and who relish hearing themselves talk, are most likely to get to the top and therefore most likely to be influential.

Now, this isn't greatly dissimilar from politicians. Having a massive ego and all-consuming ambition has always made ploughing down the opposition easier. Politicians, however, have to face voters at regular periods. Unless they head military dictatorships, heads of state have to curb their narcissistic self-interest and unbridled love of power and status to keep their jobs.

There is a quid pro quo. We vote for them (thus maintaining their narcissistic rule) if they force themselves to take enough of the public interest into consideration. This is a challenge for narcissists, who don't just think they are the most important person in the world but, according to psychiatrist M. Scott Peck, the only person in their world. Business leaders, particularly entrepreneurs, are not subject to the checks and balances which apply to publicly elected leaders. As long as they keep making money, business leaders can, and do, pretty much sing to their own hymn sheet.

> **❝What is fascinating is that we so readily buy the con. We are so keen to believe that there are right answers and clear formulae for success.❞**

We love winners, although we prefer them to harbour at least some humility. With a good spin doctor, even the most extreme narcissist can appear to be caring. If a narcissist is rich and powerful enough, he or she can afford to employ an army of PR consultants, publicists and spin doctors to make the narcissist both famous and popular.

What is fascinating is that we so readily buy the con. We are so keen to believe that there are right answers and clear formulae for success. We are so ready to believe that these answers and formulae are known to the rich and famous. Maccoby explains that as the pace of change increases, so will uncertainty. Most people hate ambiguity – they want to be shown clear ways forward by credible leaders. In such times, people with wisdom and insight know that there is no one way forward. Only narcissists, totally sure that they are the answer, dare posit simple solutions. Desperate for certainty, many people follow like lemmings, giving the narcissists the adulation they desire and the followers the illusion of comfort.

A more realistic answer is for all of us to realise that times are uncertain and that we need to work together to find mutually workable answers. This is reflected in much of the emerging leadership literature, which is about being a wise, strong and judicious leader of people. However, such leaders need mature followers. In uncertain times a good number of us regress. Instead of using the times as an impetus for growth, we seek instant answers – answers narcissistic leaders are only too happy to give us. The problem isn't with the leaders, it is with us the followers. If we choose not to see through the hype, if we choose to distract ourselves with the wonderfully professional performances provided by the narcissists, we simply get what we deserve.

Questions to ask yourself

1. What qualities do you most admire in a leader?
2. What qualities do you most dislike in a leader?
3. Can you see any of these good or bad qualities in yourself?
4. What can you do to develop the ones you like and address the ones you don't?

six

SPIRITUALITY IN BUSINESS

Making room for spirituality

There is a growing hunger for spirituality in business.

*I am certain that after the dust of centuries
has passed over our cities, we, too will be remembered
not for victories or defeats in battle or in politics,
but for our contribution to the human spirit.*

John F. Kennedy

In the 1980s, when I set up my business, I faced a conundrum. I had discovered through personal experience and study that if individuals only work for superficial, hedonistic reasons such as money, status and power, they grossly underperform and have little incentive to tackle thorny, ethical or humanitarian issues. When people think past their own petty ego to the good of the group, the whole organisation, whole society or, even more powerfully, to a force greater than themselves, they are emboldened to take risks, to be more creative, give better service and go the extra mile.

In the 1980s, talking about spirituality in the workplace wasn't compatible with making a living, so I found ways to disguise these ideas in language, concepts and programs more acceptable to business. I guess I adopted the Clayton's approach: 'The drink you are having when you're not having a drink', as the old advertisement went for the non-alcoholic drink.

In the past few months I have been asked to address no less than six conferences on spirituality in leadership. One request came from the Australian Heads of Independent Schools, whose biennial conference was entitled 'Leading with Soul'. Another came from the International Coaches Federation, who asked me to speak on 'The Spirit and Soul of 21st Century Coaching'. Others were from companies that found, through staff surveys, that spirituality in business is the topic of guidance most sought.

> **Good spiritual practice at work profits the bottom line, benefits the community and feels great.**

In their fascinating book, *A Spiritual Audit of Corporate America*, Ian Mitroff and Elizabeth Denton state that while most people feel negatively about the concept of religion in the workplace, there is a growing hunger and cry for spirituality at work. The authors defined spirituality as a sense of meaning and purpose. Their research found that people gained meaning and purpose at work through (in order of importance):

1. the ability to realise their full potential as a person
2. being associated with a good/ethical organisation
3. having interesting work
4. making money
5. having good colleagues/being of service to humankind
6. being of service to future generations
7. being of service to the immediate community.

Organisations from The Body Shop to Rank Xerox are searching for ways to provide their workers with an increased sense of meaning (spirituality) through their work. They are doing this for diverse reasons, including the company's leaders having deep religious convictions, or having a need to increase corporate creativity and profitability.

Of course, some people are sceptical of talk about spirituality in business. Mitroff and Denton found that many people to whom they spoke were terrified to express more of themselves at work. 'They were afraid that if they did express their souls, they would end up selling them to their organisations,' explained the authors.

My own experience has shown that there are unscrupulous leaders who will use any movement – be it total quality, re-engineering or spirituality – to maintain control and to manipulate people in less than ethical ways. I have also found that many leaders are hungry for meaningful work and keen to create a company in which they are proud to work and from which they obtain satisfaction. Additionally, I have found that when companies create a culture that allows people to experience, express and use their intelligence, emotions and spirit, a situation is set up in which individuals win, the company wins, shareholders win and the community wins. In other words, good spiritual practice at work profits the bottom line, benefits the community and feels great.

Questions to ask yourself

1. What does spirituality mean to you?
2. What do you think are some benefits of encouraging spirituality in the workplace?
3. How could you bring more spirituality into your daily work life?

Converting death jobs into living work

Making a positive difference is nourishing for the soul.

'Is your work big enough for your soul?' This challenging question was posed by Matthew Fox in his revolutionary book *The Reinvention of Work*. Most jobs, Fox tells us, are death work, the performance of which actually stunts the human spirit. Because industrial society is designed around the concept of a machine, most jobs are focused on the needs of the machine (system) and most people work as cogs in the wheel. This has led to the rape of the natural environment (of which holes in the ozone layer, shocking air, water pollution and deforestation are just a few symptoms) and neglect of endemic social problems, such as poverty, family abuse and discrimination. The end result is that some people get financially richer and we all end up spiritually and emotionally poorer, while passing on to our children and grandchildren a seriously ailing planet. All this assaults our souls and leaves us feeling alienated and tired. As a result we are driven to increasingly addicted behaviours, relationships and societies.

> **By choosing to make a difference we can improve the quality of our own lives and make a positive contribution to society and our planet.**

Fox is not alone in his warnings. There is a flood of books about work addressing this same issue, such as *Calm at Work* (Wilson), *Success with Soul* (Pozzi et al.) and *The Hungry Spirit* (Handy) – all of these address the effects of Fox's 'death work'. Fox, however, provides a much more radical (and dauntingly challenging) answer, the implications of which could reform our society beyond current recognition. Fox suggests that we convert our death jobs into living work. This involves several steps.

Step 1

Realise that we are all connected and that if we hurt our environment or each other, we hurt ourselves. Conversely, by not looking after ourselves we are damaging the whole of which we are part. While this philosophy fits into the great mystical traditions it is also in line with the findings of modern scientists, especially those working in the areas of systems theory. This theory states that everything is connected to everything else. Chaos theory tells us that even slight changes in one part of the system can lead to massive changes elsewhere. We need to develop a way of seeing things that takes this interconnection into account and uses this truth as a basis for our code of conduct.

Step 2

We all need to do our inner work. This means raising our spiritual and emotional awareness and working on our emotional sore spots and Achilles heels. This will make us safer people to be around and help us to see things more clearly. Lack of awareness and emotional immaturity blur our vision and make us project our own limitations, fears and failings onto the world we see.

Step 3

Link our work with our own needs, the needs of our families, the needs of our society and the needs of our planet. Fox calls this our outer work. This involves building relationships and choosing to engage in collective action.

In short, by lifting our own personal game and choosing to make a difference we can improve the quality of our own lives and make a positive contribution to society and our planet. This will lift our spirits and help us regain hope for our future as we work to improve the earth and society that we will leave to our children's children. This is work that stretches our souls. This is living work.

Questions to ask yourself

1. What connections do you see between yourself, your environment and others – examples being the air you breathe, the water you drink, your community relationships, your work relationships?
2. When in your daily life do you notice this connectedness between yourself, others and your environment?
3. What could you do to help yourself become aware of this connectedness more often?

Spiritual healing

The road to paradise is cobbled with tough lessons about our relationship to the world and each other.

In September 2000, I was in one of eleven buses blockaded by several thousand protesters as we tried to leave the World Economic Forum's Asia Pacific Summit 2000 to go to a nearby hotel for dinner. Police risked their lives to protect us from the mob, people were frightened, objects were thrown, windows were broken. Hours later we were on our way. People were furious with the protesters. But the demonstrators had a message, and we needed to listen.

We live in a global society with global problems. The polar caps are melting. The oceans are swelling due to global warming. The UN Global Environment Outlook 2000 report states that natural disasters, such as floods, cyclones and droughts, are becoming more frequent and their effects more severe. We have eradicated thousands of species of animals and plants and are having a go at ourselves. Since the end of World War II more than 50 million people have been killed by war. Globally, 1000 soldiers and 5000 civilians die every day. Deaths from tobacco, estimated by the World Health Organisation (WHO) at more than 4 million per year globally, are expected to rise to 8.4 million by 2020.

In 1950 the French scientific journal *Science et Vie* surveyed people to see what they thought the world would be like in 2001. With the promise of labour-saving devices, rising productivity, and scientific and medical breakthroughs, the prediction was for paradise. In the 1950s those who did paid work (mostly men and single women) put in around 40 hours a week. Now, except in a few European countries, the average middle manager works between 60 and 70 hours per week and spends more time travelling (locally, nationally and internationally). Then people go home to tend the kids and do family chores. Scarce private time has been stolen by mobile phones, faxes and emails, which accompany us to the bathroom, bedroom and on holidays.

Today, we are tired, stressed and depressed. The WHO suspects that within the next decade one in five people worldwide will be suffering from depression. Power and wealth does not protect us from these ills. We live, explain Danah Zohar and Ian Marshall in *SQ: Spiritual Intelligence, The Ultimate Intelligence*, in a spiritually dumb culture. Even the word 'spirituality' frightens some people. This is not surprising in a highly materialistic culture that likes to believe that we, humankind, are in control.

> **High spirituality increases our energy levels, the success of all our relationships (particularly our more intimate ones) and our sense of peace and joy.**

Oscar Wilde told us in *De Profundis*, published in 1905 (quoted in Moore):

> *...as the Greek oracle said, to know oneself: that is the first achievement of knowledge. But to recognise that the soul of a man is unknowable, is the ultimate achievement of wisdom. The final mystery is oneself.*

Spiritual wisdom is about knowing who you are, your life's purpose and that you are living your purpose. Deep spirituality is about facing and using suffering, facing and transcending pain, and having the capacity to be flexible. Spiritual people have a deep awareness of the interconnectedness of people, with each other and with their environment. They are reluctant to cause harm to others or to the environment. Spiritually intelligent people not only know how to adapt successfully to their changing environment, they have the capacity to redefine boundaries and create new, appropriate and successful paradigms.

High spirituality increases our energy levels, the success of all our relationships (particularly our more intimate ones) and our sense of peace and joy. Developing spiritually demands raising our awareness about our motivations, basic beliefs and emotions, and reflecting on our actions, our relationships and the world around us.

All of this takes time, usually very quiet time – time that most of us don't think we have. Yet, mysteriously, as we make time for meditation, reflections, journal writing and spiritual guidance, huge amounts of activity seem to become irrelevant. We have fewer crises and more hours. We feel more in control. If making money is what matters to us, we even do that more successfully.

A deep basis for any form of spirituality is a capacity to hold open the possibility that we, with our own petty egos, are not the limit of the universe. For some this is experienced by being in nature, for others by being with those they love, while others still find it in some kind of spiritual practice. Ultimately it is a form of humility.

Try it. Go for a long, slow walk somewhere beautiful – smell the flowers and leaves, listen to the birds, soak in the beauty. Sit down with those you love and drink in their smiles, their chatter and their love. Read a special poem, a spiritual tract or quote, and reflect upon it. Quietly receive the wonder that there is much you do not know. Therein lies an energy, a creative force and a sense of wellbeing that can take you to a place you have not yet contemplated. Your possibility for joy, love, happiness and personal fulfilment is as infinite as your capacity to accept the mysterious.

Questions to ask yourself

1. What do you think your life's purpose is – that is, what meaningful contribution do you have to make to society with your unique talents and skills?
2. Are you living out your life's purpose?
3. How could you live more in alignment with this purpose?

The heart is just as smart as the brain

Tap into your heart intelligence to find greater happiness and improve your relationships.

In their book *The HeartMath Solution,* Doc Childre and Howard Martin reveal their fascinating research concerning the intelligence of the heart. Part of an interdisciplinary team of scientists, doctors and psychologists who have been studying the relationship between the brain and heart, Childre and Martin provide scientific proof for what smart people have known intuitively for centuries: the heart is just as smart as the brain, and really clever people are able to access both heart smarts and brain smarts and put them together. (In my book, *Approaching the Corporate Heart* I call this weaving of brain and heart intelligence 'braiding'.)

Childre and Martin tell us that the heart communicates in four ways: neurologically, hormonally, biophysically (through waves) and through its own electromagnetic field. Heart intelligence is more intuitive, has greater perspective and has the capacity to moderate stress and improve our relationships and our health.

In line with their scientific bent, the authors summarise their research in an equation.

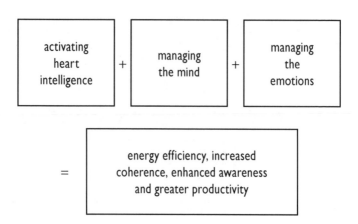

Reading *The HeartMath Solution*, I thought back over the years to all the people I have worked with who violently resisted any opportunity to activate their heart intelligence and manage (or even acknowledge) their emotions. I was again struck by how idiotic it is to try to run any business – particularly large, complex, global enterprises – without activating heart intelligence and managing our emotions. Only relying on our brains and our visible behaviours (competencies) is like going through life sitting on our hands, or riding a bicycle using only one wheel. You can do it, but why would you bother and how much more effective can you be using all your faculties – all the equipment that is available?

> **❝The metaphor of the machine that has dominated the industrial era has so imbued our thinking that we have been blinded to our own psyches (mind, spirit, soul and emotions).❞**

Travelling back from London recently, I spent several hours watching documentaries on the in-flight video system. Each one was an account of how Western medicine and science is discovering that the mind, the emotions and our energy systems are crucial parts of our effective functioning as healthy human beings and as a society. There is a groundswell from all the major disciplines letting us know that by sticking exclusively to the rational, visible and measurable parts of reality we have greatly limited our potential for success, health and happiness. HeartMath is another milestone in the journey of getting us limited industrial-age beings to see what ancient sages and traditional medical practitioners have known for centuries: there is more to us human beings than we have been prepared to admit.

The metaphor of the machine that has dominated the industrial era has so imbued our thinking that we have been blinded to our own psyches (mind, spirit, soul and emotions). Thankfully, the science we trust so implicitly is catching up with ancient wisdom and letting us know that neither are we machines nor are relationships or society mechanistic. Once we accept this reality, we open up a whole new way of operating that increases our potential for healthy success to levels most of us can't even begin to envisage. The rediscovery of the psyche will be as revolutionary as the discovery of the microchip.

Questions to ask yourself

1. Do you feel that you listen to your heart as much as your head when making decisions?
2. What do you think the advantages might be of listening to both your head and your heart?
3. How can you put more heart-opening practices into your life, such as meditation, creative arts, yoga, prayer, spending quiet time in nature, doing community work, training a kids' sports team, being part of a community?

Affairs of the heart

Success in life has a lot to do with your heart.

Back in 1998 when I wrote my book *Approaching the Corporate Heart*, a client, the managing director and owner of a successful Australian-based multinational, told me, 'Men won't buy it. They feel too vulnerable about the word "heart". It's like being in love, you lose control.'

Like it or not, our society looks down on those who wear their hearts on their sleeves. And those who let their hearts rule their head are not seen as wise, smart or likely to succeed. At the same time, we flock to movies about courage, such as *Braveheart*. We know that King Richard was brave because he was said to be lion-hearted, whereas we shy away from those who are hard-hearted, knowing that they can be cruel and unreasonable. Yet someone who is soft-hearted is unlikely to make sensible business decisions.

❝Heroes of all time have been people with heart.❞

As a hobby, I motivate a schoolboy rowing team. I started working with the team because my son was in it and it was losing. When my son left school, I stayed on with the team. About three minutes into a six-minute rowing race, rowers experience intense pain. That pain continues until they cross the finishing line, when they often collapse from exhaustion, effort and pain. To be a racing rower takes great courage. When the pain starts, the half-hearted want to give up. To win a rowing race, you have to really put your heart into it, push through the pain and go full-bore for your goal.

The first year I worked with the team, they finished the season in second place. The second year I worked with them they came second in each race. Every week we would visualise their desired goal, work on the beliefs that were blocking attainment of their goal and build relationships within the team. Each week they came second.

One day they filed in for their session with me and I could see in their faces that they couldn't take it any more – this woman was going to get them all fired up yet again, get them excited about the prospect of winning, but deep in their hearts they knew that they were going to be disappointed.

A colleague of mine had recently done a course in sports psychology. The main message was, 'get used to disappointment'. Sportspeople have to give their all every time they compete, but in every competition only one competitor or team can win. All the others have to learn, regroup and be ready to give it their all next time around.

So the rowing boys and I had a session on disappointment. We discussed how, when you really go for a goal, you have to go for it with heart and soul. If you don't succeed, you feel broken-hearted. When you feel broken-hearted you often feel like giving up, or at least giving a little less. Half-hearted rowers don't win rowing races. So we all faced, acknowledged and let go of our disappointments.

The next week, the boys made school history by becoming the Schoolboy National Rowing Champions. Their hearts jumped for joy. But the rowing season wasn't over. They still had to compete in the Head of the River, which is the pinnacle of the rowing calendar. Their school hadn't won Head of the River for 28 years. They went in fully trained, emotionally and spiritually on the money, the all-time favourites – and came third.

I was at a family wedding the day of the race. When I received the news I was shocked. What had gone wrong? I could see the boys' faces in my mind and I mourned their disappointment. Then I remembered the words of Napoleon Hill in his all time classic, *Think & Grow Rich*. Based on the study of high achievers, such as Henry Ford, Thomas Edison and Andrew Carnegie, Hill wrote:

> *All who succeed in life get off to a bad start and pass through many heartbreaking struggles before they 'arrive'. The turning point in the lives of those who succeed usually comes at the moment of some crisis, through which they are introduced to their other selves.*

I saw my broken-hearted boys not as losers but as great achievers of the future. Having the courage to be disappointed, and to feel their disappointment, was the training ground of the greatness that lay ahead.

I thought back to my disheartened MD and realised that those who feel too vulnerable to work with their hearts are misguided. Rather than weakening us, our hearts are a great source of strength. Heroes of all time have been people with heart. This MD himself was a man of great courage and heart. He had not only founded and successfully led a huge organisation but had given back big-time to the community through his sponsorship of the arts, his work with indigenous people and by establishing a not-for-profit organisation to support those with life-threatening diseases.

Perhaps it is not true that we are afraid of being folks of great heart. Maybe we are just afraid to admit it.

Questions to ask yourself

1. What pursuits/activities/relationships do you put your whole heart into?
2. Think of a heartbreak that you have experienced when you were working towards a goal wholeheartedly. Did you feel the

pain of this heartbreak and keep going towards your goal or did you give up at this point for fear of more heartache?

3. How would you deal differently with this heartbreak if you could relive it?
4. What growth/learning/positive outcomes have come from this experience?
5. How do you want to approach disappointment in the future?

Spirit doesn't get a lot of airplay

It's amazing how much can be achieved when there is a spirit of community.

Volunteering recently at my son's school, I was surprised to discover that, although my co-worker's son had left for university several years before, his father continued to organise one of the school's major fundraising activities. Given that most schools can't get parents to volunteer at all, I was curious about his ongoing interest. 'It's the spirit of the place,' he told me. 'I just love being here.' He wasn't alone.

Every time I turn up to help out there are more helpers than jobs. This makes the task pleasant. We always have time to chat – to get to know each other. We belong to a community. So we turn up in the hundreds. Shop owners, painters, consultants, engineers, doctors, farmers, insurance salesmen, mums, dads, sisters, brothers, grandmothers and grandfathers, all helping out for free. Now, as someone who is interested in leadership, I can't help but be intrigued. Most people have to be paid to work.

How much better off would we all be if more places did have a spirit, did create community and did encourage people to give for the good of others?

Pondering this I come back every time to my co-worker's words, 'It's the spirit of the place'. It's the spirit of the community that attracts people to donate their valuable time again and again.

Last week, selling at the school's art fair, I met a grandmother who had been volunteering at the school for 40 years. 'It's the spirit of the place.' How many places of work have a spirit that invites people to be part of the community? How many places of work bring so much to people that they come back for decades, voluntarily, just to help out? How much better off would we all be if more places did have a spirit, did create community and did encourage people to give for the good of others?

What is it about my son's school that builds spirit? Well, everything. As a new parent waiting outside the headmaster's door I was drawn to the full script of Martin Luther King's famous 'I have a dream' speech, in which he talks about each person's capacity to make the world a better place. Each time I attend an assembly, rally or parent's ceremony, I am encouraged to be grateful for what I have (my health, my family, my ability to enjoy life) and reminded that not everybody is so lucky. While we celebrate current successes we are reminded that people in our community are ill, grieving or suffering in some way. We are encouraged to open our hearts, to be joyous and compassionate. 'It's the spirit of the place.'

Many years ago, working with David Judd, then Operations Manager of an Alcoa Aluminium Smelter, I saw this spirit operate in a large industrial site. David believed that people should develop their own personal potential and work for the good of the whole community. He role-modelled this behaviour and then laid out the path for others to follow. He celebrated his own good fortune (through photography, bush camping and relationships) and worked for the community – setting up a creche, a gym, a medical centre, bringing Don Burrows into town to teach the local kids jazz, bringing international speakers to talk to the local people, putting the community through a personal development program, encouraging smelter staff to work with the homeless, sponsoring environmental projects, etc. When you walked onto that site you could feel the spirit of the place. It sort of hummed.

People wanted to be there. People cared – about themselves, each other and the plant. Consequently, industrial accidents decreased. Productivity increased. Absenteeism fell to nothing. Staff turnover halved. Demarcation became a non-issue – people wanted to help each other make the place as good as it could possibly be. Tradespeople who normally lined pots, volunteered to paint and garden when their normal duties were done. Engineers did secretarial work and secretaries learnt how to use tradespeople's tools. There was a spirit of cooperation and community about the place. It became a world benchmark in its industry.

In our highly rational world, spirit doesn't get a lot of airplay. Pity!

Questions to ask yourself

1. Where do you experience the spirit of community?
2. What is it that you value about this community?
3. What do you contribute to this community?
4. How could you build more community in your life?

Human nature can be improved too

We can all reach more of our potential if we put the effort in.

For years people have told me that my ideas are too idealistic, that there is little point in working towards having people optimise their emotional, spiritual and intellectual potential, to expand and enhance their behavioural repertoire. I am often reminded that people have always lied, cheated, coveted what belongs to others and resorted to bad behaviour as the result of jealousy and just plain malice. Greek and Roman mythology abounds with examples of inherent human weakness. The great god, Zeus, was always cheating on his jealous wife, Hera. Zeus went around raping maidens, Hera followed close behind laying curses on anyone who had taken Zeus's fancy.

Where would Shakespeare have been without human frailty? It was greed, pride, infidelity, jealousy and madness that underlay most of the bard's best work. We now have a whole school of psychology – evolutionary psychology – that goes to great lengths to convince us that much antisocial behaviour is rooted in our genes and is a necessary part of our human genetic inheritance.

❝Humans are constantly pushing past their own limitations in every area to which they apply their energies.❞

Personally, I think much of this 'it's only human nature' stuff is a cop-out. Once it was thought it was only human to die in what we currently consider to be mid life. Then the wonders of modern medicine took our understanding about human physical potential (assisted by new technology) to new heights. Renaissance Man was a 'pre-artificial intelligence' phenomenon – now the amount of information available to the average citizen makes us all look like geniuses compared to our ancestors. Advances in nutrition and training methods have seen us break sports records in every field. Humans are constantly pushing past their own limitations in every area to which they apply their energies.

Now, that last little phrase is actually the clue to it all. You see, we find it worthwhile to invest in curing disease, finding ways to hold back ageing, and push past all sorts of physical limitations. As a society, we find the increasing literacy, understanding and knowledge of people an economic necessity, so we invest heavily there too. Doing something about human nature is a much lower priority.

While the desire for spirituality has reportedly never been higher, our attendance at church, synagogue or mosque is on the decline. Wisdom is less important to most of us than making money and having fun. Health we will work for, and pay for (particularly if we have a brush with illness). Knowledge we will strive to gain because there is economic benefit in doing so. Being a better person, however, isn't too high on most people's agenda.

The apparent conundrum here is that we can't improve on human nature because of human nature. To argue this way is equivalent to saying we can't stay healthy because we get sick. Many years ago I went through a period where both my children and my father were very unwell. Being healthy myself, I was able to nurse all three. One day I became worried. 'What,' I asked my family doctor, 'would we all do if I fell ill?'

'You would come to me,' he replied, 'and I would make you better!' What a relief! We are not limited by our own humanity. We can make it better. We are only limited by our unwillingness to do so.

Questions to ask yourself

1. What do you believe are untapped parts of our potential as a human race?
2. What are some untapped parts of your own potential?
3. What can you do to develop this untapped potential?

Developing wisdom

*It's a shame that our society does not encourage
the development of wisdom.*

On a recent trip to the Netherlands I was surprised to notice the number of people in their 80s and 90s being pushed around in wheelchairs by people in their 50s and 60s. Visiting the tulip gardens at Keukenhof, or wandering through a picturesque village, there was a constant presence of older people being taken out into society by others who cared for them. Despite this, I noticed that many of them didn't look happy. 'Perhaps,' I mused, 'it is such a usual occurrence in Holland that people have come to expect it.' My husband thought that perhaps the unhappy-looking Dutch oldies had had a hard life and didn't feel very happy, despite the graciousness of those taking them out. So I told him about Father Harris.

Father Harris was about 90 when I met him. He was in a retirement complex for Jesuit priests. I only met him about ten times, but I can't remember ever seeing him when he wasn't smiling. As one of his carers commented, he had a remarkably cheerful disposition. One day while eating a particularly bland meal with him, he commented on how wonderful the food tasted. With a little bit of inquiry I found out that just eating regularly was a treat for him. He had spent decades imprisoned in China. While in prison his guards threw a handful of rice at him each day. He spent the rest of the day picking up the grains and eating them.

That he had survived at all was miraculous; that he had come out with such a hopeful and positive attitude was beyond belief. By the time I met him, he had many ailments which made it very hard for him to be fully mobile, yet every day he would walk about the length of a block and back. It took him somewhere between 30 and 60 minutes to cover this distance, but he did it, always smiling. As his death approached, to my eyes Father Harris became almost translucent. He had a great faith and to my mind his spirit had already returned home to its maker. His body was just taking its time to catch up.

> **Wisdom can be one of the great joys and gifts of ageing, but it takes work.**

We live in an age that has an obsession with youth and beauty at a time when we face major problems that require wise leadership. Native peoples had a tradition of leadership by wise elders. However, just as not all young people are beautiful, not all old people are wise. Some young people these days, who are dissatisfied with how they look, put themselves under the surgeon's blade. Gaining wisdom takes a little more effort. Wisdom can be one of the great joys and gifts of ageing, but it takes work. Some people just become more tired and bitter, while others, such as Father Harris, mellow into shining examples for all of us.

How do we develop wisdom, celebrate wisdom and tap the wisdom for the betterment of the planet? I believe the answer is rather unfashionable. Father Harris was surrounded by other men of the cloth, most of whom had just got old and many rather grumpy. What made him different was his great sense of faith and hope. His fellow priests had spent their lives doing good deeds, they had made a huge contribution to society. Father Harris, however, had done all that and more. Perhaps during his imprisonment he had been forced to come face to face with his own vulnerability and humanity. He had learnt to accept himself in all his imperfection and find hope and faith in something beyond the physical.

I am reminded here of Nelson Mandela, who also emerged from a time of extended isolation and hardship wiser, stronger and more full of hope. In their book *SQ: Spiritual Intelligence, The*

Ultimate Intelligence, Danah Zohar and Ian Marshall wrote that we live in a spiritually dumb society. They suggest that wisdom, lateral thinking and happiness come when we develop our spirit, embrace our hardships and grow through them.

Questions to ask yourself

1. Think of a wise person you know. What can you learn from this person about wisdom?
2. What can you learn from this person about how you can develop more wisdom in your life?
3. What pieces of wisdom do you think might most benefit you in your life right now?

seven

WOMEN IN BUSINESS

Women's participation
proven beneficial

The blending of people with ethnic,
racial and sexual differences is needed
to keep an organisation alive.

The Women's Movement, some male commentators are telling us, has done women a disservice. It is claimed that, mesmerised by the excitement and fulfilment of challenging work, some women feel cheated when seeking to have children to find they are no longer fertile. One conclusion people draw from this is that Women's Liberation has blinded women to the fulfilment of their 'true' natures.

This is an interesting perspective. From where I sit, what the Women's Movement has done is given women choices. Women can now vote, maintain a job after marriage, and combine motherhood with building a career. Women can now, and do, rise to positions of power in business, politics and academia. Choice has always brought with it responsibility and the need for self-knowledge and wisdom. The fact that some people are unhappy with the choices they have made hardly makes choice itself an unattractive option.

The liberation of female contribution has not just opened up alternatives for women but also for employers, voters and consumers. Women, by virtue of their different socialization and make-up, think and act differently from men. Smart organisations know that, in rapidly changing environments, creating an environment in which different perspectives can be tabled and harnessed is the way to ongoing learning and the kind of constant renewal that leads to sustained success. The blending of people with ethnic, racial and sexual differences is never easy, and can be particularly uncomfortable for those who previously made up the dominant cultural group. However, this discomfort might be exactly what is needed to keep an organisation alive.

> **To keep their incredibly scarce and valuable female executives, organisations are going to have to reorganise to become the kinds of places where women can healthily exist and thrive.**

For many years IBM was exceptionally proud of its cultural uniformity. Jokes were rife about the blue-suited IBM clones who set the pace in the computer market. The dominance and uniformity of the IBM culture was seen as one of the key factors of its success. Then the market changed dramatically. IBMers who were used to looking unitedly in the same direction continued to do so. The problem was, it was the wrong direction. Margaret Wheatley, in her fascinating book, *Leadership and the New Science*, tells us that to remain healthy and to function to optimum performance in chaotic environments, all systems must self-organise. This involves voluntarily throwing themselves open to the environment to ensure a constant flow of energy, relationship and information, both within the system and between the system and the world in which it operates.

The Women's Movement has made 50 per cent of the population available to organisations with the wit to capitalise on women's energy, skills and insight. Smart employers understand and utilise the difference women bring. The problem is, the women don't stay. Organisations have an appalling rate of female attrition. The numbers of female executives in large organisations are actually decreasing, which simply means that women are exercising their options. To keep their incredibly scarce and valuable female executives, organisations are going to have to reorganise to become the kinds of places where women can healthily exist and thrive.

This means that the holders of the dominant culture will need to look at how they currently think and act, not out of some ideological platform, but because it makes good business sense to keep any organisation open to its environment and in a constant state of self-organisation – continually growing, changing and including new ideas, information and standpoints, thus ensuring its success and survival.

Questions to ask yourself

1. What do you think organisations can gain by accepting and valuing ethnic, racial and sexual differences?
2. How do you relate to people in your work and personal life who are from a different background than yourself, or are of the opposite sex? Is this celebrating diversity?
3. What do you think you can learn from people who are different from yourself?

Women on top

*Women who don't want to play the male business
games need to embrace their uniqueness and
find their own way to career success.*

In their book *Smashing the Glass Ceiling,* US writers Susan Golant
and Pat Heim (1995) advise women wanting to make it to the top
in the corporate world to learn to play the business game like a
man. 'Unfortunately,' they say, 'business is still a man's game.'
Some of the advice includes:

- attend important meetings, even if they bore you to tears
- bizzare, illogical requests (such as working on weekends)
  may be loyalty tests – as long as they are not illegal or
  immoral, accede to them
- if you're torn between listening to your heart or your
  supervisor, go with your supervisor – they hold the key
  to your next evaluation and therefore your success.

**❝The tide is turning in the business world:
men are now trying to acquire the skills
most women take for granted.❞**

Golant and Heim reason that, in the short-term, we have to play
by men's rules; when enough women have made it to the top, we
can then change the system.

What rot! In my experience, women who get to the top by behaving like men have a vested interest in the system remaining just the way it is. Female executives who have sold out to male values are rougher, meaner and more competitive than any man. They know how to play by the existing rules – why would they want to change a game in which they are the winners?

Aspiring women have several options:

- they can emulate men (thereby sacrificing their own femininity and integrity – and probably their right to a happy marriage and children)
- they can choose to settle for a less rewarding career than their male counterparts
- they can find a new, creative way of getting to the top – if you don't want to play by men's rules, but still seek career success, you're going to have to make your own rules!

A woman's competitive advantage

One of the really useful things I learnt at university was that people are different from each other. You learnt to concentrate on your competitive advantage and unique strengths. In marketing jargon, products have a unique selling proposition; so have people. The theory is that by being different you can become an expert in your own distinctive way, which sets you apart from your competition. For example, Christian Dior® and Sussan® both sell women's clothes. However, they do it very differently and sell to different people because there is room in the marketplace for them both. Dior® concentrates on prestige and uniqueness, Sussan® on price and turnover.

If you don't want to play by the men's rules, but still seek career success, you are going to have to make your own rules.

It is the same with women and men. Women and men *are* different. We think differently and see things differently. If we try to compete with men on their territory, we are not concentrating on our competitive advantage. It's like Dior® charging less so that it can compete with Sussan® – it just doesn't make sense. As a minority in the corporate world, women can choose to think of themselves as Dior®. We can concentrate on our uniqueness and charge a premium for it.

In women's favour

Networking skills
Women are natural networkers. They are great at using technology to keep in touch with large numbers of people, experts at passing on information (it used to be called gossip), and have great people skills.

With the growing complexity of work, no one person can make it on their own. We need to divide tasks between specialists. With increasing amounts of work being 'outsourced' or done by subcontractors (often from the home or a small business office), we need contacts to whom we can refer work that is complementary to, but different from, our own. Women know how to keep in touch, discern and value individual differences, and match people to tasks. The voluntary sector is a great example of this. Most managers find it hard enough to get people to work for money, let alone for free. Yet for years, women have been organising people to donate their time and skills to charities, preschools and social causes.

Lateral creative thinking
We have all seen the new mother bouncing the baby on her knee, talking into the mobile phone while peeling potatoes for dinner. Women have an amazing capacity to do many things at once. Studies into the differences between male and female brains show that women have more interconnections between the right and left

lobes of their brain, which suggests they can actually process a range of complex, diverse information simultaneously. In a world of growing complexity, this is a skill male leaders are racing off to learn at training courses. Women's 'scatterbrain' mentality is, today, called an ability to think laterally.

Just when women are learning the rational male games, men are lining up to learn traditional female competencies. 'Women's intuition', for example, is now a highly sought commodity by leaders of both genders. The amount of information an executive needs to process daily is too great to be handled just rationally, bringing intuition well and truly into fashion.

> **Women's 'scatterbrain' mentality is, today, called an ability to think laterally.**

The studies on the quality of managers suggests that traditional managers (mainly men) are rigid and crusty in their ideas and behaviours. That female 'problem' of being 'fickle' has been re-framed as being flexible and creative – both essential competencies for leaders of tomorrow.

Balance

Managers around the world are being encouraged to put more balance into their lives. Men are excellent at narrowing their focus behind a limited number of objectives and investing all their energy into those things that will lead to success. This myopic vision is what has propelled them to the top. However, it is killing them in great numbers. Men suffer from all the major fatal illnesses, such as heart disease and cancer, at a younger age than women. The more women behave like men, the more likely they are to suffer the same complaints as their male counterparts, who are all running off to stress-management courses and developing their nurturing side in order to stay sane and survive.

Emotional awareness

What about women's tendency to be emotional? Increasingly, studies are showing that women's ability to empathise with others is a valuable skill.

The changing nature of work makes it imperative that people learn to operate in a team. Organisations where the employees are valued as people with feelings, needs and desires are pushing ahead, particularly in areas where service, customer relations and creativity are imperative.

It seems ironic that at a time when traditional female skills, attitudes and behaviours are becoming increasingly valued in the business world, women are still being encouraged to give up the very things in which they have a decided competitive advantage.

Steps to being successful as a woman

1. Discover your unique competencies

Work out the personal characteristics that set you apart. For example, do you have a strong sixth sense about people and situations? Can you get the kids off to school (with a packed lunch) and blow-dry your hair while building your partner up for a big interview? Have you organised the preschool fruit roster for the past four years?

These are valuable and marketable skills. Start noticing just how skilfully you live your life. The more you value yourself, the easier you'll find it to market your competitive advantage.

2. Market your competitive advantage

Reframe your skills into business speak. The sixth sense can be called innate discrimination – an ability to foresee and plan for unseen contingencies – or highly developed intuition. Your family-management skills can be presented as:

- strong ability to train and delegate (the kids now make their own lunches)
- ability to handle complexity, ambiguity and chaos
- ability to inspire and lead others.

If you can organise volunteers, you obviously have great people skills and all the makings of a hot-shot salesperson.

3. Research your niche market
Now that you know how fantastic you are, you need to find out which jobs and employers are going to use and value your unique difference. Go to the library, ask people you know, join a women's network, ask questions. Think and use your nous to work out what you want to do, how you can make money doing it and who are the best people to sell to. Find out all you can about these people. Work out the best way to let them know what you have to offer and why they will be better off with you than without.

4. Develop a strategic plan
Now stop and work out exactly what you want in life. Marriage? Children? Friends? Travel? Creative pursuits? Sport? Culture? Career? Work out how you would like to balance all the things you want. Then look through your research to find the best way to manage your career so that you will have the time and energy for living life on your terms. This will narrow down your options to a manageable level. Then explore the two or three most promising alternatives more fully, bearing in mind that you have a right to be you and to have it all.

5. Put your plan into action
Start taking action. Once you have worked out what you want, you are simply going to have to summon all your courage and go after it. Even doing one thing a day towards having what you want puts you on the path to success. It's your life – don't waste it.

Questions to ask yourself

1. Write down the personal characteristics and skills that set you apart from others. How could you reword these skills into marketable 'business speak'?

2. Research the organisations you think will most value these skills and where you think you can add the most value. Which ones appeal to you most?
3. Write and then implement your strategic life plan, ensuring you capitalise on your competitive advantages. How are you going to support yourself on this journey?

Abuse of power is unacceptable

Abuse of power can undermine the integrity,
trust and relationship that organisations need to thrive.

Recently I worked with a client who had been the victim of sexual harassment. This normally confident, assertive woman, a senior executive in a major corporation, had fallen to pieces. She suffered from stomach pain and burst into tears at the drop of a hat. She had difficulty making decisions she would normally have made in an instant. Meeting her harasser every day made it impossible for her to go to work. So she resigned.

The actual harassment was not dissimilar from something I experienced some years ago. My response to the incident, however, was markedly different. I found it instructive to review why.

A few years ago, I accompanied a woman in distress to a railway station. It was late at night. As we waited, a man in his late twenties, obviously mentally limited, came up and asked me to marry him. When I jokingly refused, he dropped his trousers. Concerned for the already suffering woman beside me, I told him to 'put that thing away' and threatened to call the police unless he behaved himself.

My client had suffered a similar embarrassment. The difference between our experiences was that her flasher wasn't a simpleton but her boss – a man supposedly of high intelligence and some standing in the community.

❝Sexual harrassment needs to be dealt with swiftly and effectively when it happens.❞

The key difference in our experiences was about power and breach of trust. The woman's boss was abusing his position of power over his employee and breaching the trust necessary in any employer/employee relationship. Also, highlighting the issue of power, it was the employee – the victim – who left. The executive was not fired. His power had allowed him to abuse with impunity. I wonder if lack of consequence will encourage him to harass someone else, and what messages will be sent across the organisation? While everyone is working hard to keep the incident under wraps, people aren't fools – they will work out that something has happened and pick up the vibes on some level. What level of integrity, trust and relationship can that organisation expect in the future?

Sexual harassment needs to be dealt with swiftly and effectively when it happens. Yet, the secret is to do whatever is possible to prevent it from happening in the first place.

Questions to ask yourself

1. Have you ever experienced somebody abusing their power?
2. How did you deal with this situation at the time?
3. In hindsight, is there a more constructive way in which you could have dealt with this situation that would have been more empowering for you?
4. How would you like to deal with such incidents in the future?

Changing the image of Cleopatra

Powerful women bring with them a new way
of seeing things and acting on reality which is
a valuable asset for any organisation.

I recently attended a university study day called 'A day with Cleopatra', which traced the image of Cleopatra from its historical origins through the depiction of Cleopatra in art, literature and film. What became evident is that Cleopatra was highly intelligent (speaking nine or ten languages), politically savvy, shrewd and charming. She was a woman who wielded great power. She wasn't, it turns out, very beautiful. During her liaison with Marc Antony, she was in her late 30s and more matriarch than seductress. Yet through art and film Cleopatra has been stripped of her intelligence, wit and political brilliance and turned into a siren of unsurpassed beauty. A key exception here is Cleopatra as depicted by Shakespeare. Although the bard wrote *Antony and Cleopatra* after the death of Queen Elizabeth I, he had written most of his work under the reign of a woman who was as clever, astute and powerful as the Queen of the Nile.

Unfortunately, at most other times, the only legitimate power available to women has been through their sexual allure (or as mothers). So in the face of resounding proof to the opposite, Cleopatra has been transformed into a scantily clad, ravishingly beautiful seductress. Ho-hum. What is it about a legitimately powerful woman that leaves many men so terrified that they have to either erase her power or transform it into sexual allure? Why is it that the only power men want women to have over them is linked to reproduction or sex?

> **What is it about the difference that powerful women often bring to a situation that makes many men want to cause them to disappear?**

The female leader in a government agency reported anecdotally of leaders who dismissed women because they didn't fit in. The leaders apparently had no criticism of the effectiveness of such women, merely that women were different and therefore best let go because they didn't fit easily into the team. What is it about the difference that powerful women bring to a situation that makes men want to cause them to disappear? Is it that female power is not only different, but more of a threat than these men are able to tackle? Is it that powerful women bring with them a new way of seeing things and acting on reality that is both effective and challenging in its difference? Women confined only to sexual power are constrained to stereotypes in the private world and effectively excluded from the public realm where their difference could prove too challenging and too effective for their male counterparts.

What many men perceive as the threat of female effectiveness has never been greater than it is today as we move out of the machine (industrial) age into the e-world, where relationships are of increasing importance. Perhaps the only way men feel they can compete with women is to exclude them from the competition altogether, or to make the rules so discriminatory against them that they come to the battle exhausted.

Questions to ask yourself

1. What positive contribution do you believe powerful women have to make to the business world and society?
2. Do you feel uncomfortable around powerful women? If so, why? What can you do about this?
3. What support do you offer to powerful women? Is there any way that you could be more supportive?

Face value

Why do business people hide their emotions
when a little animation can work wonders?

On a recent flight, a man in his early thirties struck up a conversation with me a couple of times, both before and during our boarding. After too many long-haul flights, I tend to avoid most in-flight conversations and so I was fairly non-committal in my response. When we landed, this man moved quickly across our small aircraft to the window on the terminal side and started waving and smiling. The sheer joy and excitement that emanated from him was the strongest public display of emotion I had seen in years. I looked out the window to see a young woman with rings pierced through her eyebrows, her belly button, her ears and her nose. In her arms was a beautiful girl of about two years of age. Both the woman and the girl seemed just as excited to see my fellow-flyer as he was to see them.

I found this family scene both touching and puzzling. Why was it so long since I had seen someone so happy and excited? What is it about the world of business and leadership that encourages people to mask their emotions so they operate on what appears to be automatic pilot, behaving more like robots than fully alive human beings?

Some years ago I invited a marketing specialist to attend one of my speeches to give me pointers on how I might improve. To my great surprise, she had little feedback about content but a lot to say about my 'aliveness'. She made it very clear that if I insisted on laughing, brimming with passion and bursting out of my skin with energy and life, I simply would not be taken seriously by the captains of business and government who are my market. What is it, I wondered, about being humourless and emotionally dead that encourages people to think we are important, powerful and wise?

> **❝What is it about the world of business and leadership that encourages people to mask their emotions so they operate on what appears to be automatic pilot?❞**

During the 1996 US elections, I was given some insight into this mystery. In a television interview with US novelist Norman Mailer, explaining why the Republicans so hated Clinton, Mailer remarked, 'It's easy if you're dull and boring to hate those that are alive and interesting.' Mailer believed Clinton was just too smart and emotionally alive for his opponents to tolerate. Funny, isn't it? We want our entertainers to be alive (the public, wanting entertainment, loved Clinton) so we can live vicariously through their public and tumultuous lives (much like reality TV). Yet we want powerful people – political leaders, for example – to be different.

By dehumanising our leaders (or encouraging them to dehumanise themselves) we can keep them at a distance and guiltlessly blame them for all the ills of the world. Dull and boring leaders can be cast as the Rock of Gibraltar, the steadfast parent, the immutable persona of power. If our leaders appeared to be alive and enjoying themselves, how could we forgive them for having it all – power, money *and* happiness? We can allow film stars money and status because we all 'know' that their marriages won't work and they are secretly miserable underneath. We don't even want our leaders to enjoy high spots. They would be too enviable if they had managed to accumulate power, money and stay emotionally alive.

I am avoiding the temptation here to link lack of 'aliveness' with maleness, which we also associate with power. While women may display emotion, at least we know that there are social mechanisms in place to ensure they rarely reach positions of power, and that if they do, the media will ensure they don't stay there very long.

A recent television program covered a NASA experiment where a group of men and a separate all-women group were stranded in the desert without food or water and had to find their way to a certain spot (without outside help) over a period of several days. The men worked together seamlessly. They quickly took roles, developed a plan and navigated a route. They were composed and efficient, impressive to watch. The women were a mess. They constantly got lost (map-reading has to be a sex-linked gene). They fought amongst themselves. They complained. One of the women was almost completely blind, and this slowed the women down even more. They were a straggly, chaotic bunch.

Interestingly, however, both groups achieved the task – the women, along with their blind member, did get there a little later. Even more interesting were the initial tests that showed the men were far more stressed than the women. All the emoting the women had done seemed to have cleared their emotional systems. They mightn't have looked as stitched up as the men but they achieved the goal – and will probably live longer!

And maybe that's the point. By insisting that our leaders are emotionally numb, we unconsciously push up their stress levels, thus ensuring we won't have to put up with them for too long!

Questions to ask yourself

1. Do you sometimes feel like you are living on automatic pilot?
2. Are there times when you feel emotionally, spiritually and mentally 'alive'? What helps you to feel this way?
3. How can you support yourself to feel 'alive' more often?

eight
PERSONAL
DEVELOPMENT II

Starting to grow before things become unbearable

Disasters can be great opportunities
for learning and growth.

In my experience people will go on living out the same pattern of thought, behaviour and emotional response until things get so bad and the pain becomes so great that they are forced to overcome their own inertia and transform their lives. While this may involve fighting or dropping out, it can also involve being dropped into life and into society in a more enriching, empowering and fulfilling manner.

Many years ago, I had a relentless series of disasters. My marriage failed, my daughter developed a life-threatening disease and had an arrest (her heart stopped beating and she stopped breathing). My father began a slow cancer-induced decline. Although I was a single mother with no family support or alternative income, I gave up work to nurse my father and my daughter and to tend my young son. I did these things in a very conscious and aware way. I entered into intensive personal development using my current problems as a source of deep personal and life learning.

> **Hardship, discomfort and sacrifice had been my teachers.**

Things were so bad I could give up, fight the world and become a victim, or I could take full power and full responsibility for my situation. I believe I did the latter. My daughter got better, my father died in peace, and I went back to work a wiser and more capable person. In the process I grew in dimension. I was a bigger person at the end of that year than at the beginning. I had learnt about myself, about life, about relationships. I had learnt the value of giving, of being more, of stretching past all my limits. Hardship, discomfort and sacrifice had been my teachers.

I look back on that period as a blessing. Whenever I hear of people facing hardships, I consider they have a wonderful opportunity upfront. They can use the struggles of life to be more, to grow, to give, and to move to new levels of awareness and capacity. They are on the threshold of all they are capable of being. The question is, do they have the courage? My choice was easy – things just got too bad for me to stay the same. Those made of braver material start growing before things become unbearable.

Questions to ask yourself

1. Think about a time when you made a big change in your life. What was it that inspired you to change?
2. Are there any changes that you currently wish to make in your life?
3. How are you going to motivate yourself to make these changes?

Feel and know your emotions and act appropriately on them

Emotions provide us with energy that can be used to raise us to new heights.

Often when I am approached by people wanting to bring change into their organisations they are surprised when I suggest that real change is an emotional as well as a cognitive process. People need to process their emotions as well as new ideas if they are to transform the way they operate.

Sally was a chemical engineer selected by her organisation to spearhead its strategic change process. She had isolated the key issues, pinpointed the most effective processes and was looking for a way to help people change their attitudes. She found the idea of dealing with emotion a bit off-putting. 'Change agents like me are pushed and pulled in every direction,' she noted. 'What would be the use of becoming more aware of how we feel; it would just be too uncomfortable.'

That, of course, is the point. Most of us shy away from uncomfortable emotions, yet emotions are a great source of energy, and none more so than uncomfortable ones. Discontent, impatience and anger are wonderful motivators for radical change. In the therapy of victims of domestic violence, for instance, having people feel what it really feels like to be abused provides a massive impetus for constructive action. Abused spouses and children will return again and again to their tormentors until they allow themselves to feel the pain and indignity of being bashed and having their rights denied.

The energy in these supposedly 'negative' emotions can activate us to rise out of lethargy and take the steps necessary to start a new life.

> **Again and again I find that, when people listen to their fears, doubts and disappointments, they find within themselves the hope and determination to steer a new course.**

The same is true in organisations. People will go on doing the same things until they feel the full force of the emotions associated with being ineffective, irrelevant, attacked or exploited. If properly harnessed and channelled, emotions provide the energy to reskill, upgrade relationships and learn to grow and adapt to change in positive, self-enhancing and organisationally enhancing ways.

Again and again I find that, when people listen to their fears, doubts and disappointments, they find within themselves the hope and determination to steer a new course. When we feel what it really feels like to be bypassed, undermined or shafted, we can be shaken out of our complacency with sufficient force to find new, constructive ways of operating. This, of course, takes a very real kind of courage. Those who master this courage find they react more quickly to situations, are infinitely more proactive in their approach and also see their relationship skills improving.

Most of us reject the notion of feeling our feelings because we have seen others express their emotions inappropriately. We have been the victims of people dumping their anger or using their fear to escape facing up to real issues. The problem, however, isn't the emotion. It's the way the emotion has been expressed.

Mature, effective adults learn to feel their emotions, understand the information their emotions bring and harness the emotion's energy behind the appropriate action.

Questions to ask yourself

1. Are there any emotions that you tend to avoid? Why?
2. What benefits do you think these emotions might have to offer you?
3. How could you use these emotions to motivate you in a positive direction?

You can't grow emotionally without at least some pain

Are you willing to feel some discomfort in order to become emotionally stronger?

I was asked recently by an ex-colonel, who now heads up an excellent leadership program, how far it was reasonable to go to emotionally stretch his leaders-in-training. He had recently employed a skilled guide to help his leaders-in-training face more of the reality of their inner world and thus grow in wisdom. Some people had complained.

I was both amused and fascinated by his question. When we send people to university we have no qualms about stretching them intellectually. That, in fact, is the job we consider universities are doing. Universities provide information, certainly, but we expect good universities to teach people to think so that they can process information and turn it into usable knowledge. To do their jobs well, universities have to stretch people's intellectual capacity past where it is when the student starts. We call this learning, education, and we give people degrees to show they have stretched far enough to pass the hurdles as they have been raised higher.

❝As a community we can't afford leaders who are emotionally underdeveloped.❞

As an ex-colonel, this man was only too well aware of the demands for physical fitness the army places on its leaders. All that running around parade grounds with loaded backpacks isn't aimed at keeping people in their physical comfort zone. No, it is aimed at stretching people past their physical limits to raise their physical fitness. The booming market in personal trainers has arisen as we pay people well to ensure we exercise regularly at a level that is uncomfortable and beyond the limits we would normally set ourselves.

I was listening to some experts discuss this on the radio recently. They were saying that research now shows that good fitness training actually damages the muscles and that it is in the healing of the muscles that the fitness of the individual grows. We don't worry about that and think it is wrong. So why, I began to wonder, when we place such high value on being stretched intellectually and physically, are we such wimps when it comes to being stretched emotionally?

'It hurts,' we say. Well, so does running up 200 stairs – regular practice for those in serious training. 'I feel vulnerable and exposed,' we plead. Well, that's exactly how many of us feel when we try to get our head around quantum physics or advanced statistical method. This is rarely, however, considered a good reason to give up. Good teachers wouldn't consider taking such complaints seriously. Few would even notice, let alone care, that their students were going through growing pains. If people want to learn, to attain degrees, they are expected to stretch. If they don't stretch they won't make the grade. Teachers are there to provide challenge and support (should it be needed).

In the realm of emotion, however, we have different rules. We say, 'Oh, it is soft stuff – what does it have to do with leadership anyway?' But surely emotions are no softer than ideas. As stretching intellectually allows us to turn information into knowledge, so comfort and skill with our emotions allows us to turn knowledge into wisdom. Yes, like stretching our brain or our fitness level, growing emotionally is likely to hurt. When it does we are likely to complain. When we complain, people can encourage us to give up or they can support us to move through the discomfort to new levels of emotional fitness, wisdom and emotional skill.

This, of course, will demand that we have expert teachers and good support available. Leaders need to be fit on every level. As a community we can't afford leaders who are emotionally underdeveloped. We especially can't afford leaders who are so emotionally crippled they won't even put in the effort to stretch to new levels of wisdom and maturity.

Questions to ask yourself

1. What attitude do you have towards pain?
2. How does this attitude affect the way you live your life?
3. Is this attitude serving you?
4. Is there another attitude that might be more beneficial for you?

Dealing honestly with failure

We can work for success and learn from failure.

The other day, as a community service, I ran a workshop for a group of unemployed professionals. People who had been retrenched (sometimes up to three or four times), people whose businesses had failed, people who had moved countries and been unable to find work in their new home. The group was open and searching. They had seen a side of life for which their education and upbringing had not prepared them. Their faces were stripped of the defensive armour I see so often covering the corporately successful.

It occurred to me that these people had a great opportunity before them. They could use their temporary hardship as a lever to open the door to a richer life. My mind went back to other people and other times. I remembered the radical transformation that had taken place in one client when he faced the reality that he had life-threatening cancer. He used the experience to reassess his values and his lifestyle. This self-reflection allowed him to set even higher goals for himself and his organisation, which he took to the heights of world recognition before he died. He had used what might have been a disaster as a springboard to enrich his remaining time and leave a legacy of great value to others.

❝Nobody wins all the time.
We all have good and bad times
in our lives, at work and at home.❞

I notice that many of my clients find it hard to accept it when things don't go to plan in the world of business and government. There are so many pressures on them to succeed, to get it right every time, to be in control and win. I also know that nobody wins all the time, that we all have good and bad times in our lives, at work and at home. We are the most divorced society in history, we can all expect to face a bout of unemployment at some time in our careers, and it is highly likely that we, or someone we love, will suffer from drug addiction, alcoholism or psychological illness during our lifetime.

Usually when these things happen we try to deny them, push them underground, cover them up, lest we face public disgrace and humiliation. If people know that we have 'failed' in one part of our lives, perhaps they will use it against us, deny us opportunities or judge us harshly. We all have the experiences that reinforce this fear.

Yet there is another way, a middle ground, perhaps. In the privacy of our lives we can use the good and the bad to grow in wisdom and peace. We can work for success and learn from failure. We can build around us a base of supportive people, who we trust enough to share the reality of our lives – people who can help us use the truth to grow towards maturity, peace and increased success.

In my work I have been lucky enough to help a number of top teams of large organisations to create sufficient safety in their relationships to make reality a way of life. In these organisations it is accepted that people have strengths and weaknesses, successes and failures, and it becomes safe for them to use their strengths and weaknesses to grow personally and professionally. When people stop hiding the negative and use it to move forward, problems are quickly surfaced and resolved. Relationships flourish in ways that motivate and inspire people to increased success. As an organisation's elders grow in wisdom their decisions improve, they spot opportunities and challenges early and feel secure enough to take calculated risks. Wise organisations grow and become rich because they are able to deal honestly with failure.

Questions to ask yourself

1. Do you feel comfortable to acknowledge your failures as well as your successes? Why?
2. What do you think you can learn from your failures?

Envy

It pays to know how to handle it.

The movie *Gladiator* provides us with a wonderful illustration of both good and bad leadership. Maximus, the head of Rome's northern armies, is a man of great character, devoted to his country, his men, his family and his gods. He achieves outstanding results while winning the loyalty, love and respect of his people and his Caesar. When Caesar dies, it is Maximus's great strength that wins him the envy of Caesar's heir, who sets out to destroy Maximus.

Envy is such an unfortunate emotion. While jealousy is about wanting something that someone else has, it also encourages us to be more, learn more and achieve more, spurring us on to self-improvement, hard work and focused goal-setting. Envy, however, is very different. It's all about *not* wanting someone else to have or enjoy something that you don't have and enjoy. Envy is not about having – it's about undermining, destroying and punishing someone else.

Professionals are often the subjects of envy. Few people want to put in the long hours, years of study, professional development and hard work that makes an outstanding professional. Many, however, are envious of the income and status that professionals earn. Ironically, they can also be envious of the results that good professionals achieve.

**❝We often don't expect envy
or even think we are worthy of it.
It is very puzzling – the better you
become, and the more adequately
you manage someone who is envious
of you, the more envious they
are likely to get.❞**

Early in my career, I headed up a change program in a large government agency that was being privatised. Upon my appointment, the board announced that half the agency's staff was to be sacked. It said it hadn't decided which half, but they would let people know within six months. For many of the people in this government bureaucracy, their world was shattered. They had joined the government for security and were now faced with total uncertainty – knowing they would be sacked would have been preferable to not knowing. The organisation was thrown into turmoil, and staff succumbed to health problems brought on by stress.

My response was to set up two informal networks across the organisation. One was a telephone tree, which was a way of getting information quickly to as many people as possible. The second was a series of support systems to help manage the stress. We located within the organisation anyone who had ever been a telephone counsellor, church advisor or support-group mentor and set them to work helping people contain their stress and continue to do their jobs.

I then worked with the top team to generate strategies and communication systems to ensure a smooth transition through the change. Within six weeks the organisation was running like a top. It was at this stage that my client, the head of strategy, stopped talking to me. When I asked her why, she replied tersely, 'You have managed to achieve in six weeks what I have been unable to achieve in six years.' She never spoke to me again.

This was an early lesson for me about envy. I had thought that by doing my job, she as my employer would look good and be pleased. She felt that my competence had outclassed her. Her only desire was to undermine what I had achieved – and me.

Envy is like that. In *Gladiator*, the old Caesar feasts on Maximus's success. He takes it as a sign of Maximus's loyalty. He relishes his part in Maximus's development and receives Maximus's achievements as gifts. But the young Caesar sees Maximus as all that he is not and will never be. Everything that Maximus achieves is a threat, a reminder of his own inadequacy.

Envious people are a problem because their intention is to ensure you fail. You need to manage envious people as you would manage a life-threatening disease. If you have diabetes, there is little you can do to cure it. The best you can do is manage it – you take your insulin regularly, watch your diet and follow the doctor's orders. Those with life-threatening diseases learn to understand the dynamics of their disease and manage it appropriately.

Like a disease, envy can creep up on you. We often don't expect envy or even think we are worthy of it. It is very puzzling – the better you become, and the more adequately you manage someone who is envious of you, the more envious they are likely to get. Once you realise what the problem is, you can watch them closely and ensure you take whatever steps you need to keep them in check. It's a bit like managing a naughty child. You know that they are acting irrationally, that if you give them power they will make choices that are unlikely to be wise. So you limit their power and their choices, and treat them kindly but firmly.

If, as in *Gladiator*, the envious person is in a position of power over you, this is even trickier. The best thing you can do is get out of the situation as fast as you can. If you can't do that, you will have to gather your political forces to ensure that others protect you. You will need to win protectors and supporters so that you are too strong to take on directly. It's tiring and time-consuming, but envy is like that. That is why it's called the green-eyed monster.

Questions to ask yourself

1. Have you ever been the target of anyone else's envy?
2. How did you manage this situation?
3. What did you learn from this situation about yourself and others?
4. If you could revisit this situation, would you do anything differently?

Dealing with fear

*Logical arguments are of little comfort
to people in distress.*

Why are they so emotional?' Bob, the managing director of a large engineering company, was asking himself.

It was two weeks now since he started having trouble in union negotiations. He had gained the cooperation of the union hierarchy and most of the men on the site, but then a small breakaway group began threatening the negotiations. With exasperation, Bob began telling me all the rational reasons why the maverick group shouldn't behave this way. He rattled off facts and figures that he was going to use to convince them that they were wrong.

Wrong? Were they wrong? According to which criteria? Slowly it became apparent that the dissenters were probably frightened by the process. Bob knew that, but he gave me all the arguments why they shouldn't be. Could Bob produce a radical outcome with the union by taking a quantum leap in his thinking? It was time to discuss Bob's own fears.

I discovered that he was claustrophobic. As a young solider he had even spent time in the brig rather than follow orders that he go down a deserted mine shaft. What incentive, I asked him, would be big enough to have him overcome his phobia of being crushed. 'Nothing,' he assured me. 'I just want to get the hell out.' That, it seemed to me, was a pretty good explanation for the behaviour of the breakaway group. They were just 'getting the hell out' of a situation they did not trust.

❝It's pointless to thrust increasing loads of reason at emotionally driven behaviour. ❞

I asked Bob what he would do if any of his children were caught in a cave. He told me he would go in after them. In fact, he had on a number of occasions squeezed through narrow openings to fix broken equipment, but that was because it had a purpose, something that couldn't have been achieved any other way. Meanwhile, he thrust more data and logic on his union rebels and he was getting nowhere.

Coming to terms with their fear, he could get what he wanted. For example, helping them to see how the new agreements would add to their job security might diffuse the situation. Just empathising with their apprehension would be a big move in the right direction. Acknowledging that they had a right to feel the way they did, no matter how illogical it might seem to anyone else, and then working with them to find practical ways of alleviating this discomfort could build up enough of a relationship to allow for successful negotiation. Finding incentives that meant more to the rebels than their fears was another path to success.

Bob began to relax. Understanding his own fears, he began to understand the apparently nonsensical behaviour of the breakaway group. Knowing how persuasive his own terror could be and how stubborn he was when claustrophobic, he began applying his logic to find practical solutions to the union problem.

Very often we discount other people's behaviour because we don't understand it or because we analyse it within too narrow a frame of reference. When this happens we need to put on a new set of glasses. It's pointless to thrust increasing loads of reason at emotionally driven behaviour. We have to learn to speak a common language.

How often do we hurl statistics and logic at frightened people when it's more effective to deal with their fears first? We must understand emotional issues on an emotional level before we can use our logic to build a bridge of communication.

Questions to ask yourself

1. Think about times in your life when you have felt afraid. What was the most reassuring thing somebody did for you at those times?
2. What is the least reassuring thing somebody did for you at those times?
3. What can you learn from this about how to support and reassure others when they are afraid?

Facing the dark night of the soul

We must first move into a place of unknowing if we are to transform.

Continuous improvement is no longer enough. Information has become a fast-travelling commodity. Incremental improvement, while better than no improvement at all, is simply too slow. We are in the age of revolution where wealth will be provided not by knowledge, but by insight – insight into opportunities for discontinuous innovation. In today's multi-faceted world only nonlinear ideas will create new wealth. Radical innovation is the only way to be competitive.

The theme of discontinuous change is being picked up by all the top business and leadership writers and analysts. Discontinuous change is different from what went before it. By definition, it means we can't foretell the future from the past. It demands step-out thinking and innovation.

This is a very hard concept for those of us trained in the industrial era to get our heads around. We want to be trained to do better than we are already doing. Discontinuous change means we have to reinvent ourselves, our work practices and our industries, and we have to do it fast. Reinvention demands transformation. The well-accepted metaphor for transformation is morphing from a caterpillar to a butterfly. This is very different from being the fastest caterpillar in town. Transforming doesn't involve learning so much as unlearning, doing better so much as doing differently.

> **❝ Unless we give up what we know and move through a period of unlearning, unknowing and metamorphosis, we have no chance of discovering who or what we can truly be. ❞**

The big problem with going from being a caterpillar to a butterfly is the stage in the middle, the bit when the caterpillar crawls into a cocoon. Just think about being in a cocoon. First, it would be dark and cramped. You couldn't do your usual caterpillar-like things. It is highly likely that, as a caterpillar, you never even saw (or took any notice of) a butterfly and you would certainly have no concept of what it would be like to soar on colourful wings.

This cocoon period is very similar to what religious writers refer to as the dark night of the soul – a period when you can't see forward or behind you. You feel lost, directionless and far from happy. Yet unless we give up what we know and move through a period of unlearning, unknowing and metamorphosis, we have no chance of discovering who or what we can truly be. There is a long list of people and industries that, lulled by their current success, have refused to go through the discomfort of transformation. Such refusal leads to failure.

I know that when I have been through dark periods of personal and business reinvention I have felt very uncomfortable, out of control. Planning becomes very hard when you don't know who you are becoming, what you will want and how you will achieve it. As a highly goal-focused person, this for me has been excruciatingly difficult. I also know that when I come out the other side of the reinvention process, life is so much easier, smoother and in tune with the world as it transforms around me. I see the same pattern with my clients. Passing though the dark night of the soul is far from easy but well worth the discomfort.

Questions to ask yourself

1. Can you think of a time when you experienced discomfort/ unknowing/confusion/pain just before you experienced a wonderful change in your life?
2. What did it feel like to be in this difficult place?
3. In hindsight, what do you think the benefits were of being in this difficult place before the change happened?
4. If you experience such a difficult time again, how might you approach it differently?

Growing from tragedy

*Tragedies can bring people together
and strengthen communities.*

On 2 December 1999, I was sitting at home preparing to fly interstate for an important business meeting when two trains collided and seven people were killed in the mountains just outside of Sydney. Within 30 minutes of the accident, my phone rang. 'Mum,' cried my daughter, 'I've been in a horrible train accident. People are dead.'

It's funny what goes through your brain at such times. First, disbelief. Then concern. Concern for my daughter. Was she all right? For myself, how was I going to look after my daughter and make it to my meeting properly prepared? Then gratitude and celebration: my daughter has been in a fatal train crash and has survived, uninjured.

Within ten minutes I was in my car driving to see my daughter to console her. I was to meet her outside a doctor's surgery near the train crash. There she was, unharmed but shaken and grieving. Grieving for the realisation of her own mortality, grieving for the people who had died suddenly. Grieving for the despair of their families. The police asked her to go to the local bowling club to be registered as a passenger. There I was introduced to a whole new world.

As we entered the club we were met by a bevy of priests, charity workers, trauma counsellors and police men and women. My daughter had been travelling with a friend, a nurse, who had rushed to the front of the train to be of assistance, only to find mangled bodies. He needed, and was quickly given, trauma counselling. My daughter was distressed for the dead; she was immediately ushered to a table with a priest. The room was filled with shaken passengers and those there to help. There were lots of older women making and pouring tea and coffee. School children were handing out biscuits and homemade sandwiches. Rail staff were checking that everybody who had been affected by the crash was okay. In the aftermath of this disaster there was a feeling of community, of human caring and of compassion.

My daughter lives in the town where the accident happened. She and her friend were enveloped by the local community as it went about grieving the accident. My daughter attended funerals for the dead and support groups for the living.

Somehow, out of the horror, she grew as a human being and was enriched by the community of which she was a part.

> **In the aftermath of this disaster there was a feeling of community, of human caring and of compassion.**

The other day, in response to one of my articles, I received an email from a couple who live on an Aboriginal settlement. As non-Aborigines they wanted to tell me how much they had learnt from indigenous people about community. About how, by looking after each other, by feeling connected to each other and the environment on such a deep level, Aborigines had created a sense of meaning, family and community in their lives that so many of us lack. They wrote:

People regularly hold public community meetings to discuss what to western eyes are basically family matters. The social pressures and the public shaming that can arise from these meetings all help to bind the individuals in the community in a manner that has not existed in our society for the last 100 years.

They went on to say that if organisations built interactive teams, which worked towards agreed goals, then relationships could be developed that would enrich lives and increase productivity.

When we bring our humanity into relationship and work together to enhance the common good, we not only solve problems but enrich our souls. These lessons are so old. Yet in our busyness we seem to have forgotten what we can learn from those who we see as dislocated and disadvantaged.

Lessons that become so clear in times of disaster.

Questions to ask yourself

1. Have you ever experienced or witnessed the strength of community that develops when disaster strikes?
2. Why do you think that community develops so quickly at such times?
3. What can you learn from this about community building?
4. How can you apply this to your life?

Breathing properly:
a forgotten tool?

*Deep breathing promotes a greater
sense of wellbeing.*

One of the ways that I communicate my ideas is through the use of actors. Actors can have people experience new perspectives on a variety of levels in a way that is amusing and not too threatening. One of the exercises I do with the actors is to have them act out a meeting between three people who are discussing sales figures. Astute people watching this scene notice that the players are tight, nervous and frightened. Their body language is rigid and off-putting. There is very little relationship happening between the characters.

Then I get the actors to do the skit again changing just one predetermined thing. The words are exactly the same. The actors stay in the same chairs and have the same discussion. But everything is different. They appear relaxed, open and interested. They seem to be communicating and learning from each other.

When I ask the audience what was the thing that changed, they tell me body language, tone of voice and posture. Nobody so far has discovered the secret: on the second occasion the actors are breathing, on the first they are consciously holding their breath.

What is fascinating is not just the huge impact that this small change has on the actors but that nobody works it out. Actually, this isn't all that surprising. Look around you in your place of work and notice just how many people are breathing shallowly. Performers of all kinds are taught to breathe into the depth of their body, to use as much of their lungs as they can. This provides the body with oxygen, and oxygen helps us to relax, think and operate at maximum efficiency. When we breathe well, we radiate strength, wellbeing and confidence, and other people find us approachable. More than that, when we breathe properly it is easier for us to get in touch with our 'gut feeling', which is the expert's way of taking quick strategic readings of every situation and rapidly deciding the most effective way to operate. When we deny ourselves breath we deny ourselves power, physical well-being, optimum thought and appropriate, rapid response.

> **When we breathe, our minds, our bodies and our emotions can communicate better.**

Many of my clients are (or have been) outstanding athletes or top martial artists. When these people are in physical training they consciously breathe. They know that without breath they can't operate at maximum efficiency. These same folk find it quite startling when they realise that they don't apply the same principles at work. On the sports field or in martial arts exercises they breathe, in business they don't. In my experience very few people in positions of authority do.

Babies, except those with physical ailments, naturally breathe deeply. Then, some time between infancy and adulthood, we forget to do what once came naturally. Those who work in the area of somatic psychotherapy tell us that there is a link between our minds, our bodies and our emotions. One of the most potent ways of maintaining this link is breath. When we breathe our minds, our bodies and our emotions can communicate better.

This simple fact explains both why executives don't breathe and why just about every organisational culture survey I have ever read had written 'the leaders don't walk their talk' very close to the top of the list of complaints. When we breathe we give our emotions a chance of letting us know how we feel. The way most workplaces operate these days, we don't want to know how we feel, so we don't breathe. We probably worked this technique out unconsciously years ago at school or at home when things weren't going our way. The problem is, we then made it a habit and forgot we weren't breathing.

By not breathing we rob ourselves of one of the vital necessities of life so we can stay numb to circumstances that we would rather ignore. Staying numb has us send mixed and confusing messages to the people around us. It robs us of confidence and adds to our stress. It impairs our thought and interferes with our communication.

Questions to ask yourself

1. Close your eyes and become still for a few moments. Focus on your breath. Are you breathing deeply or shallowly? Several times during the day, stop and notice whether you are breathing deeply or shallowly.
2. Deep breathing helps us to connect with our emotions and own our personal power. What can you learn about yourself from your breathing patterns?
3. What practices do you do to train yourself to breathe more deeply? Examples might include meditation, yoga, breathing exercises or swimming.

nine

SOCIAL ISSUES

Creating a better
world for all

Although technology is bringing us closer
together it is also widening the gap
between the rich and poor.

At the 2nd World Congress of Colleges and Polytechnics, the theme was 'People and Technology'. As presenter of the opening keynote address I spent time researching the issues of education and technology. Wow! – what a hot topic, especially when it comes to the digital divide.

Only 2.4 per cent of the world's population use the internet, but as of November 2000 nearly 69 per cent of those users lived in the US, Canada or Europe. Six per cent of internet users resided in currently industrialising countries where 84 per cent of the world's population live. Steve Jobs, founder of Apple Computers, feels that the digital divide is just a sanitised term for poverty. Jobs considers 'the digital divide' far less of a concern than poverty.

He's got a point. The 24, 000 people who die of starvation around the world each day aren't worried that they haven't got a computer. In Africa, just getting a teacher is rare – especially since the HIV plague has killed such a large proportion of adults. Not that teacher education in the industrialising countries is so great either. In Brazil, for example, only half of the 1.5 million teachers in state primary schools have a higher-education qualification. In other developing countries, one child in three does not complete five years of education. For the 250 million child slaves around the world, just a regular good feed and basic literacy skills would be a life-saving blessing.

> ❝ **Instead of using the technology to create a better world for all, we are using it to reinforce the privilege of a few.** ❞

It seems that many of those in industrialising countries, who receive a good education, leave their country. More than 30 000 Africans with PhDs now live outside the continent, as do many educated Chinese, Indians and South Koreans.

In the rich countries, the issues are still about money. While in the US 98 per cent of public schools are connected to the internet, many have done so through sponsorship deals with major corporations. These deals come at a cost, including the display of corporate logos on textbooks and flashing ads on computers supplied by corporations, such as Microsoft and Toshiba.

Instead of using the technology to create a better world for all, we are using it to reinforce the privilege of a few. What is interesting is how slow we have been to question this trend. Jack Welch, chairman of General Electric, has famously stated, 'The secret of success is changing the way you think.' It appears we have kept our old machine-age thinking and applied it to the new technology. This is a great pity.

The new technology opens up great possibilities to unify the planet to help solve its problems. For example, there are educational institutes making their courses available free of charge over the net, and there are also websites that provide free guidance about holistic social and environmental development.

The wonder of the new technology is its capacity to spread ideas and information. What the new technology can't do is teach wisdom, compassion and judgment – these we have to learn for ourselves.

Questions to ask yourself

1. In what ways do you think that the digital divide is further disadvantaging those who live in poverty?
2. How do you think we could use technology to create a better world rather than just reinforcing the privilege of a few?
3. What positive contribution do you make to the disadvantaged people in your local community/nation/world?

Back to the future

*Times are changing and today's business leaders
should look to the classroom to prepare for the future.*

Children learn quickly and easily. They learn to ski, speak
different languages and program technology at a speed that leaves
their parents for dead. What adults used to have over children
was experience. But whether or not adults learn from experience
depends on how they think, how they learn and, more importantly,
how open they are to learning.

Combine this with the speed of change and it may well be that
our seven-year-olds are leaving today's leaders far behind.

We're currently living in two worlds: one that's dying – the old
machine age of the industrial era; and one that's accelerating and
taking over – the e-world of the present and the future. Most of
today's leaders rose to the top during the machine era, a time of
control, fitting-in and maintaining the machine. The industrial era
was based on Newtonian physics. Then machines were superseded
by information technology and we were thrown into an era where
change travels the world at the speed of light via cables. Rules are
different. Learning is different. And making sense of it requires a
new outlook and frame of reference.

> **Leaders are still hanging onto
> their past learnings, mind-sets
> and behaviours.**

The machine-age schools taught children to learn by rote. But in South Australia children are being taught to learn from experience and to learn how to change as an ongoing life skill. Change isn't some curriculum add-on. Rather, it's the basis of 'Essential Learnings' that underpin the entire teaching system for the state.

The Essential Learnings – Futures, Identity, Interdependence, Thinking and Communication – are skills children will draw upon throughout their lives so they can manage ever changing times as thoughtful, active, engaged and committed local, national and global citizens (South Australia Curriculum, Standards and Accountability Framework, 2001). Each Essential Learning helps a child develop a particular skill.

- Futures – to maximise opportunities in creating preferred futures.
- Identity – to critically understand self-identity and group identity, as well as relationships.
- Interdependence – to critically understand the systems to which lives are connected and to participate positively in shaping them.
- Thinking – to develop particular habits of mind, to create and innovate and to generate solutions.
- Communication – to construct and deconstruct meaning, and to critically understand the power of communication and its technologies.

I recently attended a think tank of business achievers where we were asked what strategies we had used to get ahead. We had been assembled as a group of 'corporate elders' so our wisdom could be tapped and passed on to younger people (especially women). The general consensus of our group was that what worked for us was conformity, fitting in, not being seen to be different or rocking the boat, not raising embarrassing issues, yet being prepared to blow our own trumpet, play hard-to-get and 'walk' when it came to pay rises and promotions. My growing concern was that what had worked for us could actually hinder the next generation.

Yet leaders everywhere are hanging on to their past learnings, mind-sets and behaviours, even fighting for the old ways which they reward and teach to the next generation. While bemoaning the pace of change, few leaders have the wisdom to unlearn what worked in the dying machine era and move courageously into the future. Even when they hit a wall or face redundancy or failure, many leaders choose to hang on to what they know and live with the underperformance, stress and illness this brings. Then they race to coaches and executive support groups, many of which teach how to do the old things better.

This is dying behaviour from a dying era. Future success demands that we, like the children of today, face the reality of change and embrace the Essential Learnings of the new era in which we live and work.

Questions to ask yourself

1. Did your school education encourage you to learn by rote (old paradigm learning) or to learn by experience (new paradigm learning)?
2. What impact does that have on the way that you now approach learning?
3. What kind of approach would you like to have towards learning?

The getting of wisdom

*It is in everyone's best interest to work
towards developing an equitable and
sustainable future.*

I was shocked to learn the other day that the richest 1 per cent of
Americans control more wealth than the bottom 95 per cent of
Americans, and that the three richest people in the world control
more wealth than the gross domestic products of the poorest 48
countries in the world. It seems that the rich really are getting
richer and the poor are getting poorer.

Krugman reports that over the past 30 years the average
American has had only a 10 per cent increase in income, while the
top 100 CEOs' average annual compensation has leaped from $1.3
million (39 times the pay of an average worker) to $37.5 million
(more than 1000 times the pay of ordinary workers). So I wonder
what the poorest 95 per cent of people are doing about it. The
answer is, they are working their butts off to become part of the
richest 1 percent.

As time goes by, they have an increasing need to do this and
a decreasing chance. History tells us that when you have huge
disparity between the mass of people and a small, highly privileged
elite, people don't put up with it forever. The French Revolution, the
Russian Revolution and the Chinese Revolution are all examples
of this, as is the recent uprising in Indonesia. History also tells us
that these revolutions, while they might replace one ruling class
with another, don't do much to fix the disparity in wealth.

> **The brave and hardy souls that seek to be wiser seem to have the nitty-gritty of business more firmly under control.**

My job is to work with leaders – many of my clients are part of that richest 1 per cent. They know that while capitalism is flawed it seems to work better than any of the alternatives. What is really heartening is that they recognise one of the reasons capitalism has lasted so long is that it has always been able to adapt, to evolve to ensure its own survival. Their concern about giant inequalities in wealth may or may not be based on humanitarian concerns. However, the smarter ones know that if they aren't part of the solution in finding a more sustainable way forward they will definitely have a big, personally threatening problem on their hands.

These wise leaders know they have to find ways of giving people a chance to equal out disparity; they have to give back to the community that has served them so well. They know they have to support international think tanks, take an active interest in and support organisations that are working towards creating a sustainable future.

Unfortunately, many people (no matter how rich and successful) are far from wise. These people want to run away from a problem that has the potential to be a time bomb. They live in houses behind high walls and suburbs patrolled by security guards. They send their children (under guard) to elite (and therefore segregated) schools, they mix in elite circles and keep their reading and listening within a very narrow range. These people are putting their heads in the sand, hoping that as the poor get poorer and therefore angrier and more resentful, they can at least be kept at bay.

But the smart ones, the real leaders, the people with vision, know we have to help the system evolve, we have to find ways of creating a more equitable and sustainable future. So they meet, nationally and internationally, formally and informally, searching for answers to vexing, complex and very challenging questions. In my consulting rooms I see them look within themselves to better understand their own motives, their own humanity and ways in which they can be part of the solution. I see them face their own demons, challenge the system that has served them so well, and grieve the problems their children are inheriting based on the failures and short-sightedness of the actions of the past. This is the getting of wisdom.

Watching my clients grapple with these problems, I know that it is personally uncomfortable for them, personally confronting and challenging. Yet they have the emotional courage and intelligence to search for real answers – to work at using their wealth, privilege and power to create a better tomorrow. These leaders want to be involved in creating a society that nurtures rather than destroys people.

Most leaders are flat out getting profits up, fighting today's fires. The brave and hardy souls that seek to be wiser seem to have the nitty-gritty of business more firmly under control. When I listen to them talk, the common theme seems to be that they really believe in human potential. They are firmly committed to supporting their staff to do their best and to lead their organisations to new heights.

There seems to be a positive correlation between wise leaders and outstanding results. Pity that more organisations don't support the getting of wisdom.

Questions to ask yourself

1. Are there any social issues that you are avoiding?
2. Why are you avoiding these issues?
3. What might you have to gain by facing these issues?

The big people are those who give

What a shame that our society does not value those who give.

In his book *The Gift*, Lewis Hyde compares gift economies (based on reciprocity – commonly found in tribal societies) and the market economy that currently dominates the Western world. He writes:

> *Every culture offers its citizens an image of what it is to be a man or a woman of substance. There have been times and places in which a person comes into his or her social being through the dispersal of his gifts, the 'big man' or 'big woman' being that one through whom the most gifts flowed. The mythology of the market society reverses the picture: getting rather than giving is the mark of a substantial person.*

This renders as valueless the gifts of those who work in the service of others – placing at the top of the social order sportspeople, the very rich, and celebrities who have acquired fame, fortune and success for themselves. The hollowness of this way of being is graphically portrayed in the musical *Chicago,* which is a witty singalong farce on how wanton crime, egotism and show business can be more potent tools for fame, fortune and influence than talent, integrity and justice.

Chicago is the story of a less-than-talented chorus girl whose aim of hitting vaudeville is achieved through committing cold-blooded murder, securing the high-priced services of a 'showman' lawyer, and using her predicament to manoeuvre her way to a modicum of celebrity that would otherwise be beyond her grasp. What I found so alarming about *Chicago* was that its message was so true. In our 'Things go better with Coke®' society we are on a constant search for happiness, youthfulness, beauty and wealth. The winners – those we emulate – are those who *have*, not those who *give*.

> **When we are tired we rest, when we are sad we cry and seek solace with a kind, giving other. When we are rich we share, when we are needy we graciously accept help. We live as human to human. So simple, so reliable, so soul-enriching.**

We want to believe there is a perfect state of wellbeing and happiness that we can and will attain if we only try hard enough, find the right help, guru, plastic surgeon or formula. We avoid (or belittle and abuse) the losers – those who are sick, unemployed or weakened in some way. They only serve to remind us of our humanity. We seek out role models who are members of the 'have' category. We defile, underpay and sue the givers – schools, teachers, nurses, nannies – and rush out to buy our latest copy of *BRW's* 200 rich list (annually, the best-selling edition of the magazine).

The World Health Organisation tells us that depression is about to become the second major epidemic facing the Western world, affecting no less than one in five people. Mother Teresa, one of the world's great givers, whose death was overshadowed by that of Princess Diana – a younger, lovelier celebrity – wrote in her book *In My Own Words*:

> *In the developed countries there is a poverty of intimacy, a poverty of spirit, there is loneliness and lack of love. There is no greater sickness in the world today than that one.*

It seems to me that all these things are connected and the answer is amazingly simple. We are all human. As such we have good times and bad times, times when we feel great, times when we feel tired, times when we win, times when we lose and times when we feel like giving up. All of this is part of being human. When we can accept these things in ourselves, we begin to accept them in others. In fact, as we begin to accept our own humanity we find it reassuring in others. Loneliness disappears as we begin to seek out people who are human just like us.

As we accept, value and celebrate our own humanity we cease to worship the rich and famous. We begin to relate intimately with other humans rather than living vicariously through larger-than-life celebrities.

As we acknowledge our humanity we start to look after ourselves. When we are tired we rest, when we are sad we cry and seek solace with a kind, giving other. When we are rich we share, when we are needy we graciously accept help. We live as human to human. So simple, so reliable, so soul-enriching. When we move into this level of acceptance we know that big people are those who give, not those who accumulate. When we value humanity we know that givers are the people of real substance.

Questions to ask yourself

1. Do you tend to pride yourself more on what you own or what you give?
2. In what ways do you give to others?
3. What value do you believe that you and others get from this giving?

Learn from Diana's example

*Princess Diana used her public profile
to make a difference to millions.*

The funeral of Princess Diana was watched by hundreds of millions around the world. Love her or hate her, see her as a brainless blonde or an astute political player who shrewdly used the media to her own ends, you can't deny that this one woman made history. Hundreds of thousands queued around the clock (often without food and subject to blistering heat and rain) to sign a book of condolence for a dead woman they had never met. We heard constant questioning of the validity of the monarchy and the suitability of the Windsor family who currently head the British Establishment.

Queen Elizabeth in her unprecedented speech to a nation in mourning was clear: Diana the woman, Diana the phenomenon, had a lot to teach us. Diana called herself a product – worth millions to the media, who used her image ceaselessly, to the charities she supported and to the fashion designers whose creations she wore. Diana was a politician, who single-handedly turned tradition on its head and raised questions others would have been too frightened to ask. Diana was a leader, who won the hearts and minds of millions around the world.

She gave people a sense of belonging, she echoed their self-doubts and mirrored their life's journey. Diana's style, beauty and royal title were invaluable in attracting worldwide attention, but interviews with grievers made it clear that it was Diana's humanity, her vulnerability and her caring that made her the

'People's Princess'. 'She's one of us,' uttered the public and politicians alike.

The Royals, doyens of traditional leadership training, were all stiff upper lip. As the piles of flowers around the royal palaces grew, one had to notice that Diana had achieved loyalty and respect that would send most leaders green with envy. Diana exemplified honesty and integrity – in so doing she made the monarchy transparent to her public, who saw behind the palace walls through her eyes. Many didn't like what they saw and called for change.

Similar trends run through the corporate world. Leaders can strip mavericks of their titles and privilege, but if the rebels are telling the truth and they have public respect, it might be the establishment that totters. Diana let people see her humanity. This laid her open to attack but allowed her to 'touch people's hearts'. Business leaders constantly maintaining a facade of strength, invulnerability and control fool no-one. Their fears simply ripple throughout their organisations, causing people to hide the truth and spend inordinate amounts of time playing politics, always putting their 'best foot forward' rather than uncovering problems and working to solve them.

> **Grievers made it clear that it was Diana's humanity, her vulnerability and her caring that made her the 'People's Princess'.**

Business leaders might choose to dismiss the lessons Diana taught. To do so would be foolish. Diana's public contains the consumers, workers and, increasingly, the shareholders of today's business leaders. If these leaders want the loyalty, commitment, power and energy that comes with world-class leadership skill, they will need to learn the nebulous ways that allow them to touch the heart of their public.

Questions to ask yourself

1. What did you most admire about Diana?
2. What do you believe that you can learn from her example?
3. How can you put this into action in your life?

What do you contribute?

Let's ask each other 'what do you contribute?'
rather than 'what do you do?'

At a party recently, I met a young man who asked me what I did. I told him that I worked around the globe with senior executives helping them grow in terms of wisdom, character and judgment, and teaching them how to use their learning to lead their organisations and communities to new levels of success and wellbeing. 'So you're in human resources,' he declared. I wasn't too happy with being stuffed into a box and labelled in such a way. I work with people, not 'human resources'. After several attempts to relocate me in other boxes, the young man lost interest and walked away.

I can't say I was displeased. He had earlier told me that he ran a website that reinsured compulsive gamblers. His website provided gamblers with the opportunity to gamble against the odds of success of their own gambling. He was an American MBA and knew all about human resource management – or so he told me. Actually, he projected the image that he knew all about most things.

Reflecting on this interaction, I realised how limiting the 'what do you do?' question is. In a society which values money, money and money, the 'what do you do?' question is really about locating people in the financial pecking order. The question really reads – is this person financially successful? powerful? useful to me and therefore worth knowing?

I have decided that a more useful question to ask is: 'What contribution are you making to society?' The underlying theme is whether this person is caring and responsible. Is this person a contributing member of society?

As I write this I am preparing to address a conference for Volunteers Australia. This is an organisation that supports those who give freely of their time and services to make our society a better place. The 'what do you do?' question to many of these people would receive a 'I'm retired' or 'I am unemployed' or 'I'm a mother' answer. The 'what contribution are you making to society?' question would elicit a whole raft of interesting information and stories that would show how this retired, unemployed, home-based person – the one who society often overlooks – is in fact someone of great substance and merit.

> **❝If we take the agenda off what we do and put it on how we contribute, we can regain our dignity and self-respect from knowing that we make a difference.❞**

I could be labelled a speaker, a mentor and the chairman of a company that runs strategically based culture-change programs. I often think, however, that the contributions I make to society come through my volunteer work with young people, community groups and as a writer. I get paid to enrich companies, I gain my personal fulfilment through enriching people's lives and building community. Someone asking me the 'what do you do for a living?' question would never discover all that.

If we take the agenda off what we do and put it on how we contribute, we can regain our dignity and self-respect from knowing that we make a difference. We can support each other in doing this by acknowledging that we are all more than a label or a job description. By asking 'how do you contribute?', we can help to change the agenda in a way that works for individuals, society and humanity.

Questions to ask yourself

1. What skills/networks/positions do you have that could help you to make a positive contribution to society?
2. How would making such a contribution benefit yourself and others?
3. What do you need to do to motivate yourself to do this?

Bibliography

Books, videos, on-line dialogues and articles

Barker, Joel, *The Business of Paradigms*, 1990.<www.joel-barker-change-management-video-training- tapes.com>

Bennis, Warren, <www.behaviour.net/column/bennis>, 2000.

Bernstein, Aaron, 'Too Much Corporate Power', <www.businessweek.com> September 11, 2000.

Breitman, Patti; Hatch, Connie; and Carlson, Richard, *How to Say No Without Feeling Guilty: And Say Yes to More Time, More Joy and More of What Matters Most to You*, Boradway Books, New York, 2001.

Cairnes, Margot, *Approaching the Corporate Heart: Breaking Through to New Horizons of Personal and Professional Success*, Simon & Schuster, Sydney, 1998.

Cambron, L., 'The CEO's Revolving Door', *Far Eastern Economic Review*, Hong Kong, vol. 165, no. 3, 24 January 2002.

Childre, Doc, and Martin, Howard, *The HeartMath Solution*, The Institute of HeartMath, UK, 1999.

Deal, Terrance, and Kennedy, Allen, *Corporate Cultures: The Rites and Rituals of Corporate Life*, Perseus Publishing, Cambridge, 1982.

De Bono, Edward, *Teaching Thinking*, Cox & Wyman Ltd, UK, 1976.

Fox, Matthew, *The Reinvention of Work: A New Vision of Livelihood for Our Time*, Harper San Francisco, 1995. Gardner, Howard, *Leading Minds: An Anatomy of Leadership*,

HarperCollins Publishers, UK, 1995.

Golant, Susan, and Heim, Pat, *Smashing the Glass Ceiling: Tactics for Women Who Want to Win in Business*, Simon & Schuster, New York, 1995.

Goleman, Daniel, *Emotional Intelligence*, Bloomsbury Publishing, London, 1995.

Handy, Charles, *The Hungry Spirit*, Arrow Books Ltd, London, 1988.

Hill, Napoleon, *Think & Grow Rich*, Ballantine Books, USA, 1960.

Hopkins, Michael, and Richmond, Tom, 'The Culture Wars', *Inc Magazine*, 15 May 1999.

Hyde, Lewis, *The Gift*, Vintage, Great Britain, 1979.

Irving, Janis, 'Group Think', *Psychology Today*, November 1971.

Kets de Vries, Manfred, *Fools and Imposters: Essays on the Psychology of Leadership*, Jossey-Bass Publishers, San Francisco, 1993.

Kiyosaki, Robert; Lechter, Sharon; and Ward, Jim, *Rich Dad Poor Dad: What the Rich Teach Their Kids About Money That the Poor and Middle Class Do Not*, Warner Books, New York, 2000

Krugman, Paul, 'For Richer', *New York Times Magazine*, New York, 20 October 2002.

Maccoby, Michael, 'Narcissistic Leaders: The Incredible Pros, the Inevitable Cons', *Harvard Business Review*, January/ February 2000.

Menadue, J., 'Whose Democracy, Theirs or Ours?', *Australian Financial Review*, 24 August 2001.

Mintzberg, Henry, *The Rise and Fall of Strategic Planning*, Prentice Hall, New York, 1994.

Mitroff, Ian, and Denton, Elizabeth, *A Spiritual Audit of Corporate America*, Jossey-Bass, San Francisco, US, 1999.
Moore, Thomas, *The Education of the Heart*, HarperCollins Publishers, New York, 1996.

Mother Teresa, *In My Own Words*, Liguori Publications, UK, 1996.

Naisbitt, John, and Aburdene, Patricia, *Megatrends*, Warner Books, New York, 1982.

Naisbitt, John, and Aburdene, Patricia, *Megatrends for Women*, Random House, UK, 1993.

Naisbitt, John, and Aburdene, Patricia, *Megatrends 2000*, William & Morrow Company, New York, 1990.

Norwood, Robin, *Women Who Love Too Much*, Arrow Books, London, 1985.

Peck, M. Scott, *The Road Less Traveled*, Arrow Books, London, 1978.

Ponder, Catherine, *Dynamic Laws of Prosperity*, DeVorss & Company, California, 1988.

Pozzi, Doris, and Williams, Stephen, *Success With Soul*, Prentice Hall, Australia, 1998.

Science et Vie, Groupe Excelsior Publications, Paris, <www.excelsior.fr>

Seligman, Martin, *Learned Optimism*, Random House Australia, Sydney, 1992.

Sher, Barbara, and Gottleib, Annie, *Wishcraft: How to Get What You Really Want*, Ballantine Books, US, 1979. Smith, Adam, *An Inquiry into the Nature and Causes of the Wealth of Nations*, Oxford University Press, UK, 1985. South Australian Department of Education, Training and Employment, 'South Australian Curriculum, Standards and Accountability (SACSA) Framework', Adelaide, 2001. Wheatley, Margaret, *Leadership and the New Science: Learning About Organisation From an Orderly Universe*, Berrett Koehler Publishers, San Francisco, 1992.

'Who Leaders Are', *Fastcompany*, Gruner & Jahr Publishing, Boston, <www.fastcompany.com>

Wilber, Ken, *A Brief History of Everything*, Hill of Content Publishing, Melbourne, 1996.

Wilson, Paul, *Calm at Work*, Penguin, Melbourne, 1997. Zohar, Danah, and Marshall, Ian, *SQ: Spiritual Intelligence, The Ultimate Intelligence*, Bloomsbury Publishing, London, 2000.

Movies

Antitrust, MGM Home Entertainment, USA, 2000. *The Bank*, Footprint Films, Australia, 2001. *Braveheart*, Fox Home Video, USA, 1995.
Erin Brockovich, Universal Pictures and Dreamworks, 2000.
The Insider, Walt Disney Home Video, 1999.
The Man Who Sued God, View Films, Australia, 2000.
Vertical Limit, Columbia, USA, 2000.

Theatre

Corporate Vibes by David Williamson, Sydney Theatre Company, 1999.

Index

Other titles by Margot Cairnes:

*Approaching the Corporate Heart: Breaking Through to New
Horizons of Personal and Professional Success*

Boardrooms That Work

*Peaceful Chaos:
The Art of Leadership in Times of Rapid Change*

*Reaching for the Stars: The Politics and Process of Bringing
Vision into Reality*

All those who wish to explore the author's services or support
her mission are welcome to visit:

Zaffyre International
www.zaffyre.com

If you wish to contact the author you may do so by email to:
mcairnes@zaffyre. com

PROOFREADING CORRECTIONS
By Leigh Robshaw & Josie Gagliano